Transforming Self and Community

Revisioning Pastoral Counseling and Spiritual Direction

Len Sperry

THE LITURGICAL PRESS
Collegeville, Minnesota

www.litpress.org

Cover design by David Manahan, O.S.B. Photo courtesy of JOHN FOXX IMAGES.

1 2 3 4 5 6 7

Library of Congress Cataloging-in-Publication Data

Sperry, Len.

Transforming self and community : revisioning pastoral counseling and spiritual direction / Len Sperry ; foreword by Keith J. Egan.

p. cm.

Includes bibliographical references and index.

ISBN 0-8146-2803-6 (alk. paper)

1. Pastoral counseling. 2. Spiritual direction. I. Title.

BV4012.2 .S665 2002

253.5—dc21 2001050249

Contents

Foreword

There is, as anyone knows, much to criticize in contemporary, post modern culture. However, Dr. Len Sperry is in no way what Pope John XXIII called a prophet of doom; he is not a mere critic. Rather Sperry's message is not only a message of hope; he makes specific recommendations to remedy deficiencies in both the theory and practice of psychology and spirituality. Despite rampant individualism, overweening narcissism and the crippling privatization of experience, Sperry offers new horizons for an exciting future in which the morass of unrelieved secularism and wishy-washy relativity can be banished from the healing arts.

For too long a time psychological theory and practice have been held hostage by a ban on concern with the moral life. Yet, have we not been restive under this ban, aware that life cannot be lived in a value-free vacuum as if what we do and how we behave do not matter? Moreover, spiritual concerns have been relegated to so private an area that they were not to be broached by those who have aspired to the helping professions. You will find, as I have, that it is nigh impossible to think in value-free terms and of life without a solid spiritual foundation once one has completed this book. Reading this work has been a refreshing mini-course that has galvanized my thinking and initiated new avenues of awareness about ways in which psychology and spirituality can enrich each other. That these disciplines dialogue with each other is imperative.

For me, more than anything else, Len Sperry argues convincingly that the transformation of the human person is not nearly complete when one has brought some peace and direction to the individual. Transformation, the actualization of the human person with all her gifts including the human capacity for the divine, is both a personal and a societal transformation. The quality of our lives depends on our relationships with other human persons and with God. Christian Spirituality that is following Jesus under the guidance of the Holy Spirit is the foundation for becoming a full, free human person whose relationships are magnanimous and life giving. With such a spiritual foundation to one's life, one's horizons are limitless. May I say infinite? The spiritual director and the pastoral counselor have the confidence that, after one has done all that one can, one is handing over to the Holy Spirit the work that can only be done by a God who has loved the human person and the human community into existence. From Sperry we learn that the human person and the human community will flourish when life has a strong moral foundation and an ever deepening spiritual direction. Moral fiber and a strong spirituality are the path to what Aristotle and Thomas Aquinas have said is the destiny of the human person and the human community—happiness. Even a glimpse now and then of eternal happiness is enough to ignite in the human heart the desire to be free and loving, signs of a truly mature life, psychologically and spiritually.

For a long time I have been convinced that friendship which is mutual growth in goodness is not only a great gift but a reliable sign of spiritual and psychological growth. Thomas Aquinas went so far as to say that friendship exists first in the triune God. Sperry urges his readers to heed the value of friendship as a spur to moral advancement. I returned more than once to Sperry's discovery that "a review of their teachings shows that Aristotle, Augustine, and Aquinas considered friendship the key to the moral life."[1] Some ethicists have even contended that morality is best rooted in friendship.

Spiritual directors and pastoral guides must not hesitate to offer a genuine hope for a quality life to those who come to them for direction and guidance. Whatever clients bring to the profes-

[1] Page 83.

sional, be they moral dilemmas, vocational crises or spiritual questions, the guide or director must offer confident guidance and effective ways to lead a more ethical life and to pursue a spirituality appropriate to one's stage of development. Like St. Augustine, every human heart is restless until it rests in God.[2] No one must blur the heights to which the human heart, with grace, may rise. Freed from obsessions and compulsions, one may live with dignity and vitality. Yet, let it be known that God can mercifully work even with frail and weakened human structures when one has done what one can to overcome one's deficits. Think of the fragile personality of Thérèse of Lisieux whom God transformed into a young woman who became not only a saint but a doctor of the church.

Len Sperry is, to his finger tips, the professional psychiatrist and spiritually sensitive and experienced counselor and director. He does not preach. Nor does he moralize in this book or elsewhere. Yet, his message is a comfort, a strength and an impetus to have the courage to pursue the good life as well as a committed spiritual life. One feels secure as Sperry shares his vast knowledge of a variety of fields, psychological and spiritual. I feel grateful that I could profit from a mind that has mastered so much diverse literature. In addition, Sperry follows on every page proven methodologies. Moreover, his theology, in particular, is grounded in the scientifically informed methodology of the Jesuit Bernard Lonergan. Sperry moves effortlessly from practice to theory and back to practice again. His book is based on solid theory and practice, and always one readily anticipates that Len Sperry will, with ease, bring one back to down-to-earth practice that has emerged from reliable theory and genuine human experience.

Although Sperry avoids moralizing, it is clear that his work is inspired by his own spiritual quest and by a deep and vital faith. Consequently I found myself not only speculatively informed but also inspired to be a better teacher and a more trustworthy spiritual director. Those results alone justify the price of this book. *Transforming Self and Community* is a fresh look at what psychology

[2] *Confessions.* Henry Chadwick, trans. (New York: Oxford University Press, 1992) 1.1.1.

and theology can do when they collaborate to dispose the human person and the human community for transformation. As I read this book, I kept drifting to those great lines of St. Paul which, look to me like a synthesis of Sperry's wisdom: "Do not be conformed to this age but be transformed by the renewing of your minds, so that you may discern what is the will of God—what is the good and acceptable and perfect will of God."[3] Transformation, personal and communal, is the goal of both pastoral counseling and spiritual direction. Ultimately, this transformation of humanity, as John of the Cross has written, is "indescribable."[4] Moreover, the Spanish mystic, like Sperry, offers hope and advocates courage even when the struggle is arduous. John of the Cross, a keen student of the human condition and a spiritual director for the Christian churches through the ages, has assured his readers: "If anyone is seeking God, the Beloved is seeking that person much more."[5]

Keith J. Egan
The Aquinas Chair in Catholic Theology
Saint Mary's College, Notre Dame, Indiana
and Adjunct Professor of Theology
Notre Dame University

[3] Rom 12:2; NRSV.

[4] *The Living Flame of Love,* 3.6. *The Collected Works of Saint John of the Cross,* rev. ed. Kieran Kavanaugh and Otilio Rodriquez, trans. (Washington, D.C.: Institute of Carmelite Studies, 1991).

[5] Ibid., 3.28

Preface

We live at a point in time and in a culture that exalts the self and at the same time wounds the spirit. It is a time of spiritual longing within a culture of narcissism and materialism. The type of self-fulfillment and transformation this culture promises is illusory and fleeting. Not surprisingly, an increasing number of adults, particularly baby boomers, are instead seeking a truer and more substantial type of spiritual fulfillment, and are turning to spiritual direction and pastoral counseling for guidance. These individuals are searching to find a deeper sense of meaning and purpose in their lives, a greater degree of spiritual and psychological wholeness and well-being, the resolution of moral concerns, as well as relief of anxiety and depression.

Unfortunately, as currently practiced, both spiritual direction and pastoral counseling tend to be only partially responsive to client needs and expectations. That is because many of the theories underlying the practice of spiritual direction and pastoral counseling are based more on psychology than spirituality, they minimize or exclude character and moral concerns, and may even unintentionally foster individualism and spiritual narcissism. What's needed is an approach to spiritual direction and pastoral counseling that is more holistic, that integrates spiritual and moral constructs with the psychological and emphasizes all aspects of transformation, including social transformation.

The Search for Wholeness and Transformation

Over the years I have taught a variety of courses involving the themes of spirituality, pastoral counseling, and spiritual direction and have practiced spiritually-oriented psychotherapy, pastoral counseling, and spiritual direction. In the past ten years I began to notice that an increasing number of individuals, including professional ministers, have sought my assistance with their spiritual and moral concerns in addition to their psychological issues and concerns. Most were also seeking to integrate the spiritual dimension in their daily lives. I too have sought to better integrate the spiritual as well as moral dimensions in both my personal and professional lives.

The question of whether my clients' requests were unique or normative was intriguing. Thus, I undertook an unofficial survey and asked several psychotherapists, spiritual directors, and pastoral counselors who were willing to talk about these matters. I inquired about what type of concerns and expectations prospective clients had in seeking therapy, counseling, or direction from them. The results of this query revealed two things. First, prospective clients, as well as ongoing clients, expressed concerns beyond the psychological and spiritual domains. Second, many of these individuals assumed and expected that the professionals they were consulting would be willing and able to assist them with moral as well as psychological and spiritual issues and concerns.

Surprised by these expectations, I searched for a published national survey data bearing on this question. Although unable to locate survey research with direct bearing on the question, I did find a survey of religious and spiritual interventions utilized by social workers. Ronald Bullis, the author of the study, indicated that over 16 percent of the surveyed therapists recommended "religious/spiritual forgiveness, penance or amends."[1] While this survey was not designed to investigate

[1] Ronald Bullis, *Spirituality in Social Work Practice* (Philadelphia: Taylor & Francis, 1996) 20.

how often clients bring moral concerns to therapists, it is clear that some clients bring these concerns and that at least some of the therapists surveyed did respond to such client concerns.

I wondered if receptivity to moral concerns has anything to do with the way therapists, pastoral counselors, and spiritual directors are trained and supervised. From my experience as both a graduate student and academician I have observed that graduate training programs in spiritual direction and pastoral counseling have focused largely on the psychological and spiritual dimensions and play down moral concerns of clients. Moral concerns seem to be inconsistent with the psychospiritual focus that most programs have adopted. At the present time, it does not appear that such training programs view an integrative approach to training—one that includes the spiritual, psychological, and the moral dimensions—as a priority.

My review of the recent literature in spiritual direction and pastoral counseling reflects a similar sentiment. Recently, while there has been an increasing number of books, book chapters, and articles published in several areas of theory and practice in both specialties, there has been little, if any, published about the moral concerns of clients. In fact, there is very little written about the moral dimension except for professional ethics and ethical guidelines of clinical practice.

Essentially, there is a disparity between what clients expect and what counselors and directors consider to be professionally appropriate to discuss. Clients seem to want to discuss and process moral issues and concerns that pastoral counselors and spiritual directors do not appear to be encouraged to deal with by their professional training, associations, or published literature. This disparity could be viewed as disappointing, but I viewed as a challenge. The challenge is to conceptualize and operationalize ways of integrating the moral with the spiritual and psychological dimensions for the practice of spiritual direction and pastoral counseling.

There was another reason for pursuing this book topic. About two years ago I became interested in the dimensions of conversion or transformation. I wondered if these dimensions of transformation would be useful in working with psychotherapy clients who were priests or pastoral ministers. The dimensions proved helpful in developing case formulations with clients who had a variety of issues and concerns, particularly religious, spiritual, and moral concerns. I subsequently published a paper describing this application. I began to wonder why there was little or no mention of these dimensions in the spiritual direction and pastoral counseling literature. Literature on self-transcendence theory came the closest to my interest in transformation, but the more acquainted I became with utilizing self-transcendence in pastoral counseling and spiritual direction the more uncomfortable I became.[2] It seemed that self-transcendence was ostensibly focused on only one aspect of transformation, personal transformation, but not on social transformation. Other theories also seemed to be exclusively focused on the individual with little or no regard for the community. Why this limited focus? It seemed that such a focus is inconsistent with the Christian message. My interest was sufficiently piqued to explore the topic in depth.

The dimensions of transformation seemed to be a useful framework for thinking about a client's functioning, but little else. Was it possible to combine the insights of these dimensions with other religious, spiritual, psychological, or other constructs to be more clinically useful? In a grandiose moment, I even speculated that a new theory for the practice of spiritual direction and pastoral counseling might emerge. I undertook this book to find answers to these various questions. The project has prompted me to read widely in not only the pastoral counseling, spiritual direction literature, but also in moral philosophy and moral psychology, moral theology, spirituality, and in critical psychology. It has prompted me to talk with several individuals who teach, supervise, or practice spir-

[2] Walter Conn, *The Desiring Self: Rooting Pastoral Counseling and Spiritual Direction in Self-Transcendence* (New York: Paulist Press, 1998).

itual direction and pastoral counseling. I'm most grateful for time and insights these wonderful individuals shared with me.

The purpose of this book, then, is twofold. First, it critically analyzes current theories underlying the practice of spiritual direction and pastoral counseling. Second, it develops and illustrates an integrative model for pastoral counseling and spiritual direction that overcomes the apparent deficits of previous theories, i.e., reductionism and narcissism, emphasis on self-development and self-transcendence. The proposed model is holistic and integrative and emphasizes both self and social transformation.

Transforming Self and Community

Transforming Self and Community: Revisioning Spiritual Direction and Pastoral Counseling provides a panoramic perspective for spirituality, spiritual direction, and pastoral counseling. This perspective emphasizes the process of transformation and incorporates recent theoretical and research developments. It provides a psychospiritual-moral perspective for understanding and respecting individuals' unique spiritual journey of development, their experiences and striving to grow and change, their strengths and achievements, as well as their developmental deficits and unfinished business. In addition, the book describes and illustrates clinically useful guidelines for the practice of spiritual direction and pastoral counseling.

The reader will be introduced to a number of exciting cutting-edge developments in spirituality which are impacting spiritual direction and pastoral counseling. These include the emergence of "positive psychology" and its research focus on human strengths and virtues; "transpersonal psychotherapy" with its emphasis on spiritual practices, new breakthroughs in object relations theory, and self-psychology; and recent research on self-transcendence and transformation. *Transforming Self and Community* describes and illustrates a holistic, integrative model which provides a common foundational basis for spiritual direction and pastoral counseling. It provides a clinically useful "map" and set of practice guidelines for assessing, selecting goals and a focus, planning interventions, and monitoring progress. In addition, it presents extensive and compelling case material that clearly describes and illustrates the integrative model in a way that is clinically useful and valuable.

This book has been written primarily for professionals who practice, teach, or are in the process of learning how to do spiritual direction or pastoral counseling. Nevertheless, spiritual seekers, clients, or prospective clients of spiritual direction or pastoral counseling may also find this book enlightening.

The book is arranged in eight chapters. Chapter 1 overviews the practice of pastoral counseling and spiritual direction, including an analysis of the concerns of individuals who seek pastoral counseling and spiritual direction. It describes trends in the current practice of pastoral counseling and spiritual direction, including the movement toward increasing professionalization and the impact of an over-reliance on psychological constructs, reductionism, and individualism on these two specialties. Chapter 2 reviews four prominent theories underlying the practice of pastoral counseling and spiritual direction. It critiques these theories and provides criteria for a more holistic and integrative model. Chapters 3, 4, and 5 provide detailed review and reflection of various constructs in the spiritual, psychological, and moral perspectives as they relate to the practice of pastoral counseling and spiritual direction. Chapter 6 presents a holistic model which integrates key constructs from the spiritual perspective, i.e., spirituality and spiritual practices; the moral perspective, i.e., character and virtue; and the perspective dimension, i.e., self and self-capacities, in relationship to the outcome dimensions of transformation, i.e., conversion. It describes and illustrates the value and clinical utility of this integrative foundation or model.

Chapters 7 and 8 illustrate the integrative model in action. Chapter 7 provides an in-depth description of a spiritual direction case. The case example illustrates the value and utility of the integrative model in terms of spiritual assessment and interventions. Similarly, Chapter 8 provides an in-depth description of a pastoral counseling case and the clinical utility and value of the integrative model. Finally, Chapter 9 summarizes the main points of the book and speculates on future developments regarding the theory and practice of spiritual direction and pastoral counseling.

A word on terminology: spiritual direction has a long and venerable tradition. However, for some, the designation "direction" connotes a relationship based on paternalism or spiritual superiority rather than a relationship based on mutuality. Accordingly, they prefer designations such as "spiritual friendship," "spiritual companioning," or simply "spiritual guidance." I view the director as a fellow traveler on the spiritual journey who mutually collaborates with the directed. Because the integrative model reflects this sentiment, I've opted to retain the traditional designation.

1

Spiritual Direction and Pastoral Counseling: Recent Trends

Today, an increasing number of individuals are exploring spirituality and searching for ways to integrate the spiritual dimension in their lives. Why is this? Many explanations have been offered, and most of these point to cultural forces. Ronald Rolheiser contends that contemporary culture has deeply wounded Americans.[1] He points to narcissism, pragmatism, and unbridled restlessness as the wounding forces. Individualism, a core feature of American culture, breeds self-preoccupation with self-fulfillment and narcissism, which is incompatible with a communal perspective. Pragmatism is reflected in our striving for efficiency, achievement, and practicality. Rolheiser indicates authentic spiritual living is impractical and inefficient. Finally, an unbridled restlessness prompts individuals to crave diversion and excitement which further desensitizes them to their deep spiritual core. Not surprisingly, such individuals are searching for ways to reverse these cultural influences.

One of the first places seekers turn for help is to institutional religion. Jean Stairs notes that "the world is crying out for the church to be more like the church, to represent the

[1] Ronald Rolheiser, *The Shattered Lantern: Rediscovering a Felt Presence of God* (New York: Crossroads, 1995).

space and place where holiness, meaning, and God can be found, experienced, understood, and reimagined."[2] Unfortunately, for some the spiritual search is compounded by "spiritual homelessness," the experience of no longer feeling "at home" in one's religious traditions or with ministers, priests, or rabbis.[3] Accordingly, many spiritual seekers, whether experiencing spiritual homelessness or not, are turning to pastoral counseling for spiritual direction. Whether they search for help within or outside congregational structures, they are seeking to achieve meaning and purpose in their lives, a sense of wholeness and well-being, and resolution of moral concerns.

Spirituality Today and the "Psychologization of Spirituality"

How can the spirituality that Americans are seeking be described? Based on surveys and discussions with spiritual seekers drawn to the Omega Institute, the largest center in the United States focusing on spirituality and wellness, Elizabeth Lesser, cofounder of the institute, has articulated what she calls the "New American Spirituality."[4] She contrasts it with the traditional spirituality which emphasized hierarchal power and provided a clearly defined path to truth and spiritual growth with prescribed spiritual disciplines, rituals, and practices. This new spirituality, which she recently renamed Twenty-First–Century Spirituality, is based on democracy and diversity and draws from religious teaching of the Christian tradition and weaves it with the wisdom of the contemplative and eastern traditions, feminism, and the findings of contemporary psychology into new forms of spirituality.[5] However it

[2] Jean Stairs, *Listening for the Soul: Pastoral Care and Spiritual Direction* (Minneapolis: Fortress Press, 2000) 3.

[3] David Steere, *Spiritual Presence in Psychotherapy: A Guide for Caregivers* (New York: Brunner/Mazel, 1997).

[4] Elizabeth Lesser, *The New American Spirituality: A Seeker's Guide* (New York: Random House, 1999).

[5] Elizabeth Lesser, "Insider's Guide to Twenty-first–Century Spirituality," *Spirituality and Health: The Soul/Body Connection* (Spring 2000) 47.

is described or named, there is clearly a therapeutic element to this spirituality.

The "psychologization of spirituality" refers to the therapeutic influence that modern psychology exerts on understanding the spiritual life.[6] Downey voices the concern that a psychologized spirituality appears "to have eclipsed the salvific as the governing category in spirituality."[7] The implications of such a psychologized, therapeutic spirituality are great. Such a spirituality gives rise to "self-absorption, self-preoccupation, self-fixation, even when the focus on the self is aimed at improving relationships with others. The criticism that much contemporary spirituality is mute on issues of social justice . . . is not without warrant."[8]

The psychologization of spirituality also exemplified reductionism, in that spirituality is essentially "reduced" to psychological constructs. Psychological reductionism is an over-reliance on and uncritical adoption of psychological constructs, such as self-fulfillment and self-realization. Intentionally or unintentionally such theories may actually promote and reinforce individualism and spiritual narcissism. This over-reliance of such psychological constructs is both ironic and embarrassing since a major reason prospective clients seek out spiritual and pastoral guidance is to neutralize and reverse the cultural pulls of individualism.

Pastoral Counseling and Spiritual Direction Today

A reasonable question can be asked: Are pastoral counseling and spiritual direction, as currently practiced, responsive to the needs and expectations of seekers? Jean Stairs notes that

[6] Brant Cortright, *Psychotherapy and Spirit: Theory and Practice in Transpersonal Psychotherapy* (Albany: State University of New York Press, 1997) 235. Michael Downey, *Understanding Christian Spirituality* (New York: Paulist Press, 1997) 8.

[7] Downey, *Understanding Christian Spirituality,* 106.

[8] Ibid., 8–9.

> many pastoral care givers are acutely aware that people are desperately seeking to make connections with holiness, the mystery of life, and the divine force of creation. . . . Protestant churches are now scrambling to respond . . . but it is clear they are ill prepared to do so.[9]

Why is this?

There are a number of reasons for this situation. Suffice it to say that the theories underlying the pastoral counseling and spiritual direction are characterized by reductionism and individualism, both of which can unwittingly foster spiritual narcissism. Subsequent sections of this chapter detail the issues of reductionism and individualism and make the case for a more holistic and integrative model for the practice of pastoral counseling and spiritual direction.

Furthermore, a domino effect of sorts results: theoretical limitations impact the nature and scope of training and supervision, which subsequently impacts the focus and practice patterns of spiritual directors and pastoral counselors. One troubling example is the matter of fees. Fee structures can effectively deny access to spiritual direction or pastoral counseling to those who are poor or of limited means. And since many pastoral counselors engage in weekly, long-term therapy and will not or cannot treat managed care clients, they effectively serve a primarily middle- and upper-class clientele.[10]

The Present Context of Pastoral and Spiritual Counseling

In this era of accountability and sensitivity to the consumer, psychotherapists are being urged to become ever more sensitive to the needs and expectations of the clients with whom they work. Presumably, pastoral counselors and spiritual

[9] Ibid.

[10] Bruce Childs, "Pastoral Care and the Market Economy: Time-Limited Psychotherapy, Managed Care and the Pastoral Counselor," *Journal of Pastoral Care* (1999) 48.

directors are also taking their clients' and directees' experience and expectations seriously and focusing their efforts accordingly. However, even though lip service was accorded to the importance of needs and expectations of clients and directees, the actual focus was likely to be the counselors' or directors' theory of therapeutic change or spiritual development *and* the practice directives learned from training directors and supervisors. In other words, theory and practice patterns were the prisms through which the experiences of clients and directees were refracted and mapped. For example, the Enneagram and stages of self-development are commonly adopted theories that influence and guide the spiritual directors, just as are practice directives such as "schedule month sessions" and "respond, don't lead" the directee. Object relations dynamics and DSM-IV categories serve a similar function for pastoral counselors. Such theories and practice directives facilitate learning to recognize patterns of behaviors and to structure the practice of spiritual direction and pastoral counseling, but they also exact a price. The price is that clients and directee are categorized and subtly influenced and shaped in the image and likeness of specific theory and practice directives.

So what are the actual needs and expectations of prospective and ongoing clients for pastoral counseling and spiritual direction? Table 1.1 lists several common areas of the concerns that individuals bring to psychotherapists, pastoral counselors, and spiritual directors.

Concerns in Category I reflect the spiritual domain of life, while those in Category III reflect the moral domain, and those in Categories IV and V reflect the psychological domain. Category I concerns are usually associated with spiritual direction, i.e., relationship with God and spiritual practices. Category II concerns include the meaning and purpose of life and discernment about major life decisions. While Category II concerns are also likely to be addressed in spiritual direction, they were the mainstay of pastoral care and counseling in the era before pastoral counseling became psychotherapeutically-focused. Recently, pastoral counseling appears to be "reclaiming" this category of concerns.[11] Furthermore, concerns listed in Category IV are typically associated with pastoral counseling, i.e., the so-called "problems of daily living": relational conflicts and issues.

Finally, concerns in Category V are typically considered the province of psychotherapy and psychiatry. That does not mean that a spiritual director would avoid these symptoms or concerns. Rather than attempting to process them psychotherapeutically, the director might ask: "Where is God for you in this situation?" to assist the client to reflect on the spiritual dimension of these symptoms or concerns.

But what about Category III concerns, that is, moral or ethical issues? In the past pastoral counselors and spiritual directors, who were often priest-confessors, would routinely deal with an individual's moral or ethical issues. Then pastoral counselors would help persons who were confused about moral choices or who had violated established Christian norms to offer moral guidance or guide them through a process of forgiveness and restoration to the community.[12] For all practical purposes, there was no separation between pastoral counseling and ethics. Today, however, contemporary spiritual directors, pastoral counselors and psychotherapists, as well as secular psychotherapists appear to be reluctant or unwilling to process moral and ethical issues with clients. There clearly is a separation or split between pastoral counseling and ethics.

[11] Israel Galindo, "Spiritual Direction and Pastoral Counseling," *Journal of Pastoral Care* 51 (1997) 395–402.

[12] James Poling, "Ethical Reflection and Pastoral Care, Part II," *Pastoral Psychology* 32 (1984) 163.

Table 1.1: Common Presenting Concerns

Category	Concerns
I	relationship with God; prayer and prayer problems; spiritual practices; discernment regarding spiritual experiences; spiritual emergencies
II	issues involving the meaning and purpose of life; discernment regarding major life decisions; issues involving self-development, i.e., growth in virtue
III	moral and/or ethical issues involving oneself; moral and/or ethical issues involving relationships; moral and/or ethical issues involving work or social institutions
IV	losses/grieving; relational conflicts; work, family, self imbalances; work/school problems; failed expectations; mild to moderate symptoms or impairment
V	moderate to severe symptoms or impairment; characterological or personality-disordered behavior; addictions; sequelae of early life trauma

There are many reasons why pastoral counselors are reluctant to deal with a client's moral and ethical issues. Prominent among these are a culture of pluralism, moral relativism, and the pervasiveness of the psychodynamic perspective in pastoral counseling. In a pluralistic society ethical statements are more likely to be understood as personal opinions rather than as the consensus of a community. James Poling notes that the "widespread acceptance of pluralism has effected dramatic changes in patterns of behavior found acceptable by the general population to whom pastoral care is directed."[13] This is reminiscent of Alasdair MacIntyre's critique of moral relativism. MacIntyre contends that the erosion of moral certainty by philosophies which ignore the idea of community or communal values leads to a society of "managers," "aesthetes," and "therapists."[14]

[13] Ibid., 167.

[14] Alasdair MacIntyre, *After Virtue,* 2d ed. (Notre Dame, Ind.: University of Notre Dame Press) 30–2.

Furthermore, the influence of psychoanalysis and psychodynamic thinking has reshaped pastoral care and pastoral counseling from moral guidance into self-exploration and self-discovery. From the psychodynamic perspective, discussing ethical concerns in counseling were perceived as moralistic assaults to the embattled ego, which fostered neuroses. The end result was that ethics became "reserved for preaching and teaching, . . . while pastoral care focuses on compassion and empathy to help individuals search their own experience, resolve their own conflicts, and decide their own norms."[15]

Since many individuals approach pastors and pastoral counselors for help in deciding what is right, best, or appropriate for their lives,[16] the challenge of pastoral counseling is to balance moral guidance with compassion and empathy.[17] Don Browning notes that entering "into sensitive moral inquiry with troubled and confused individuals without becoming moralistic is the major technical and methodological task for training in pastoral care in the future."[18] The situation is rather similar in spiritual direction. Until the early 1960s, and certainly prior to Vatican II, most spiritual direction in Roman Catholicism was provided by ordained ministers, i.e., priests. Not surprisingly, spiritual direction took on a sacramental character and the discussion of one's daily life included not only prayer and spiritual practices but also moral matters. A spiritual director was often a directee's confessor. Thus, ethics and spiritual direction were closely related.

One of the outgrowths of the Second Vatican Council was that spiritual direction became increasingly the domain of non-ordained spiritual directors. As a result, spiritual direction and ethics became increasingly separated. And, as spiritual di-

[15] Poling, "Ethical Reflection and Pastoral Care, Part II," 167.

[16] Paul Pruyser, *The Minister as Diagnostician* (Philadelphia: John Knox, 1976).

[17] Don Browning, *The Moral Context of Pastoral Counseling* (Philadelphia: Westminster Press, 1976).

[18] Ibid., 3.

rection became increasingly informed by psychology, particularly the psychodynamic perspective, instead of ethics and moral theology, the split between spiritual direction and ethics widened as it had in pastoral counseling.

So who is providing moral guidance today? Among others, advocates of moral guidance today include talk show hosts and philosophical counselors. On a mass scale, the controversial Dr. Laura Schlesinger is well known today. In a nationally syndicated daily radio broadcast, Schlesinger, a licensed marriage and family counselor, dispenses moral advice on almost every conceivable topic in her call-in talk show. On a one-to-one basis, philosophical counseling is provided by philosophically-trained individuals who offer advice on Category III concerns. Philosophical counselors can be certified by the American Philosophical Practitioners Association. Thus, in addition to dealing with Category III concerns, these counselors also offer guidance on Category II concerns, i.e., the meaning and purpose of life and discernment about major life decisions.

Over the course of several decades the specialties of pastoral counseling, spiritual direction, and psychotherapy have changed and evolved. In some specialties the degree of change or evolution has been significant. For example, it was previously noted that pastoral counseling had shifted away from dealing with ethical and moral concerns (Category III). Unfortunately, the same change has also been noted for spiritual direction.

The Current Practice of Spiritual Direction

Spiritual direction, also known as spiritual guidance, spiritual friendship, and spiritual companionship, is practiced in nearly all spiritual traditions.[19] In the Christian traditions its roots go back to the third century, and while the practice has evolved since that time in the Catholic tradition, it has vigorously

[19] Timothy Freke, *Encyclopedia of Spirituality* (New York: Sterling Publishing, 2000); R. Walsh, *Essential Spirituality* (New York: Wiley, 1999).

developed in the various protestant traditions in the past thirty years. It can be described as the art of spiritual listening carried out in the context of a one-to-one trusting relationship. It involves a trained director who guides or is a companion for another person, listening to that person's life story with an ear for the movement of the divine. Spiritual direction typically occurs in the context of prayer, and a priority is placed on discernment of spiritual experiences. It focuses on the maintenance and development of spiritual health and well-being, and assumes that the person is already whole, but has not yet fully embraced this truth for themselves. Thus, it presumes a moderate degree of psychological health and well-being. Spiritual direction is customarily provided in a one-to-one format and usually on a monthly basis, although spiritual direction can also occur in small group settings. Some spiritual directors and guides charge a fee or request a free-will offering, while others do not.

In the spiritual direction session there may be a candle, a Bible, or some other non-verbal symbol representing the Holy. A priority in Catholic spiritual direction is placed on discernment. The relationship between director and directee is one of mutual engagement based on the recognition that both are walking the same spiritual journey. The role of faith in the spiritual dimension and one's relationship to a faith community are central to Christian spiritual direction.[20] In addition, spiritual direction involves spiritual conversion, in that it is attentive to the "dynamics of change through conversion, the radical transformation, . . . a relational, personal surrender to a personal, living God."[21]

A focus on developing and monitoring the directee's prayer life, including meditation or contemplation, is the central method of spiritual direction. Instruction in prayer and the prescription of rituals and other spiritual practices are other inter-

[20] Carolyn Gratton, *The Art of Spiritual Guidance: A Contemporary Approach to Growing in the Spirit* (New York: Crossroad, 1992).

[21] Galindo, "Spiritual Direction and Pastoral Counseling," 400.

ventions. When indicated spiritual directors may refer directees with certain for concurrent psychotherapy or will suspend spiritual direction until the course of therapy is completed. Whether one professional can effectively and appropriately provide both spiritual direction and either psychotherapy or pastoral counseling is a matter of considerable debate. Gerald May believes it is improper for one professional to provide both.[22]

Before the 1960s, spiritual direction was typically provided by priest-confessors. Then, moral issues (Category III) and concerns and issues about life's purpose and meaning and discernment of major decisions (Category II) tended to be the main focus of spiritual direction. Discussion of virtue and vice as well as the sacrament of penance were commonplace. Sometimes, issues in Categories I and IV were also involved in that form of spiritual direction.

Since Vatican II spiritual direction has increasingly been provided by non-clergy, typically by other ministry personnel and lay persons who have either some ecclesial endorsement or who function as an independent providers of spiritual guidance without such endorsement. Formal training has become a norm as spiritual direction becomes increasingly professionalized. Today clients or directees are increasingly concerned about spiritual practices and their relationship to God. Thus, it should not be surprising that the focus of spiritual direction is primarily on Category I and II concerns, although problems of daily living (Category IV) may also be discussed. It appears that these same foci will continue in the future.

Currently, there is no set educational and experience requirements or certification for the practice of spiritual direction. Some contend that it is a vocation rather than a profession; a special calling for which formal coursework and supervision are not essential. Others contend that specialized training in selected areas of theology and psychology are helpful and essential. Currently, there are a number of formal graduate training

[22] Gerald May, *Care of Mind, Care of Soul: A Psychiatrist Explores Spiritual Direction* (San Francisco: HarperCollins, 1992).

institutes and programs in spiritual direction but no universally recognized certification or licensure for spiritual directors.

Spiritual direction is currently entering a stage of expansion and professionalization. Spiritual Directors International, a professional organization that claims a worldwide membership of 3,500, has begun publishing its own professional journal, *Presence,* and has recently ratified a set of ethical standards and guidelines for the practice of spiritual direction.[23] Debated questions both within and outside this organization include the matter of certification and the concerns about fees for services rendered. Spiritual direction has moved well beyond the model of the priest as director-confessor to a more inclusive model wherein professed religious and other lay persons provide the majority of spiritual direction today. In the past, spiritual direction provided by a priest-confessor model of direction seldom involved fees; increasingly today spiritual directors are charging fees or requiring donations in order to provide for their livelihood. This has led to considerable debate about fee schedules, sliding schedules and the ethics of limiting access, and the prospects that spiritual direction could be limited to the middle- and upper-class clients.[24]

The Current Practice of Pastoral Counseling

Pastoral counseling is either practiced as a brief, time-limited form of treatment that is problem-solving or solution-focused, or a longer-term form that is often psychoanalytically-oriented and focuses on personality change.[25] Clergy and other ministry personnel with some training in pastoral care and counseling provide a majority of short-term

[23] Brian Lescher, "The Professionalization of Spiritual Direction: Promise and Peril," *Listening* 32 (1997) 81–90.

[24] Tad Dunne, "The Future of Spiritual Direction," *Review for Religious* 53 (1994) 584–90.

[25] Howard Stone, "Pastoral Counseling and the Changing Times," *Journal of Pastoral Care* 53 (1999).

pastoral counseling, while ministry personnel and others with formal supervised training in psychotherapy and who may be certified or licensed practice what is often called pastoral psychotherapy. Pastoral psychotherapy is variously defined but tends to involve longer-term therapy, and in some instances is difficult to distinguish from psychotherapy.

Clergy and other ministry personnel who have some training in pastoral care and counseling provide a majority of short-term pastoral counseling. However, ministry personnel and others with formal supervised training in counseling and psychotherapy, and are certified and/or licensed, can practice what is called pastoral psychotherapy.

Clientele for pastoral counseling are typically individuals troubled with life transitions, emotional or relational crises, or because of guilt, abuse, addictions, or low self-esteem. Pastoral counseling is well suited for such crises and concerns, and is a unique form of counseling which uses religious and spiritual resources as well as psychological understanding for healing and growth.

As in psychotherapy, the relationship between pastoral counselor and client is important and maintaining some measure of clinical distance is useful in diagnosis and therapeutic change. Nevertheless, many recently trained pastoral counselors advocate a mutually collaborative relationship with the client. Treatment interventions usually include active listening and other problem-solving or solution-focused counseling methods. It may also include advice on religious or spiritual matters, that is, forgiveness. Unlike spiritual direction, pastoral counseling typically does not bring to bear the resources of the client's faith community for healing, growth, or integration.[26] Furthermore, pastoral counselors are likely to refer clients with certain presentations for psychotherapy.

Today, its primary goal is problem resolution and restoration of psychological health; however, personality change may

[26] Galindo, "Spiritual Direction and Pastoral Counseling."

also be a goal in pastoral psychotherapy. In the past, moral guidance (Category III) was a central focus of pastoral care and counseling, as were concerns about the purpose of life and discernment of major life decisions (Category II). Discussion of and advice about problems of daily living (Category IV) might also have been provided. Since the late 1930s these foci have radically changed.[27]

Currently, pastoral counselors are most likely to focus on the client's problems of daily living (Category IV) and on more complicated psychological disorders (Category V). And, although issues and concerns about the purpose and meaning of life and major decisions (Category II) will be processed by contemporary pastoral counseling, these concerns are likely to be related to the client's psychodynamics. While most pastoral counseling took place in a parish context, today an increasing amount of counseling is more likely to occur in centers, clinics, and private practices not formally sponsored by a parish or an ecclesial body.

Like spiritual direction, the pastoral counseling is currently preoccupied with becoming a recognized profession. This means that issue of training, certification, and professional identity are central concerns. An increasing number of pastoral counselors are licensed to practice, usually in a mental health specialty, and certification is available from the American Association of Pastoral Counselors. This professional organization represents three thousand pastoral counselors and is actively exploring ways of incorporating a focus on spiritual concerns (Categories I and II) and spiritual direction methods into the practice of pastoral counseling. While some are wary of extending the scope of pastoral counseling citing major differences in epistemological perspectives and praxis stances between the two fields, others are supporting this extension.[28] Needless to say, the identity of pastoral counseling is significantly impacted by such forces as managed behavioral health care and the increasing numbers of spiritual directors and

[27] Stone, "Pastoral Counseling and the Changing Times."
[28] Galindo, "Spiritual Direction and Pastoral Counseling."

mental health counselors who compete for many of the same clients as pastoral counselors.[29] Based on the proliferation of published articles and statements by leaders of the pastoral counseling profession, it appears that spirituality and spiritual issues (Category I) will become increasingly a part of pastoral counseling practice in the future.

Several trends in pastoral counseling can be noted: it is becoming increasingly professionalized, it is moving out of parish settings and into private practice or clinic settings, it is being denied access to managed care panels or limited to the lowest possible reimbursement rates, and it is increasingly competing with mental health counselors, psychotherapists, and other health providers for market share.[30] It would not be unreasonable to conclude that pastoral counselors are likely to face the same ethical challenge as spiritual directors, limiting access to services to those who can afford them.

The Current Practice of Philosophical Counseling

As noted earlier, philosophical counseling is a relatively new professional specialty. Philosophical counselors offer philosophical counseling for a range of problems or issues involving morals, values, and the meaning and purpose of life. They apply philosophical analysis in one-on-one counseling, group facilitation, and even organizational consulting.

How does this form of counseling work? Lou Marinoff, Ph.D., a philosophy professor and president of the American Philosophical Practitioners Association, describes it as a process involving a logical and analytic evaluation of the client's concerns.[31] He describes five components of the process:

[29] Stone, "Pastoral Counseling and the Changing Times."

[30] Brian Childs, "Pastoral Care and the Market Economy: Time-Limited Psychotherapy, Managed Care and the Pastoral Counselor," *Journal of Pastoral Care* 62 (1999) 47–56.

[31] Lou Marinoff, *Plato Not Prozac: Applying Philosophy to Everyday Life* (New York: HarperCollins, 1999).

(1) problem analysis, (2) constructive expression of emotion, (3) analysis of options, (4) considering and incorporating a philosophy that assists in choosing and implementing the option, and (5) achieving a new equilibrium in life.

Philosophical counselors can be certified by the American Philosophical Practitioners Association. The association is a not-for-profit educational corporation that trains, certifies, and represents its member practitioners. Certification is based on the following qualifications: an advanced degree in philosophy; documented experience in counseling clients philosophically; and professionalism and reputability of character, which they indicate includes recognizing clients who are not good candidates for philosophical counseling, and providing appropriate referrals. This certification is not licensure, and philosophical counselors cannot represent themselves as mental health counselors or psychotherapists. While some philosophical counselors have cross training in Rational Emotive Therapy or applied ethics and specialize in particular methods or perspectives, others are more general in their practices.

Since contemporary pastoral counseling and spiritual directions appear to have relinquished a focus on moral and ethical issues (Category III), it should not be surprising that the relatively recent specialty of philosophical counseling would emerge to fill this void. It appears that philosophical counselors focus on both offering moral guidance (Category III) and about clarifying life's meaning and assisting clients in making major life decisions (Category II). As more of these philosophical counselors are cross-trained in therapeutic approaches such as Rational Emotive and Cognitive Therapies—approaches that were designed to treat Category IV concerns—it would not be surprising if the focus of philosophical counseling extended to problems of daily living (Category IV).

The Current Practice of Psychotherapy

Psychotherapy is perhaps the most common of all the helping professions. It is certainly largest in terms of the number of practitioners and the number of clients involved. These numbers may be three to four times more than the number of clients involved in all of spiritual direction, pastoral counseling, or philosophical counseling combined. Psychotherapy is the treatment of choice for Category V problems. In addition, psychotherapy is also applicable to Category IV problems and concerns.

The typical clientele involves disordered clients or patients presenting with symptomatic distress and usually some degree of impairment in one or more areas of life functioning. The typical goals of treatment are the reduction of symptomatic distress and the restoration of baseline functioning. Depending on the type of psychotherapy, personality change may or may not be a treatment goal. Increased psychological well-being, self-fulfillment, or individuation may be additional goals of some psychotherapeutic approaches. Establishing a working therapeutic relationship, sometimes called a therapeutic alliance, is central to effecting change and positive treatment outcomes. The relationship can vary from situations in which the psychotherapist functions in an expert role, as in classical psychoanalytically-oriented psychotherapy, to a mutual collaborative relationship with the client. Various psychotherapeutic interventions are utilized depending on needs of the client or patient and the issues being addressed, and psychotropic medication or referral for a medication evaluation may be necessary.

It is estimated that there are approximately 450,000 licensed psychotherapists in the United States, including social workers, marriage and family counselors, mental health counselors, psychiatrists, and clinical and counseling psychologists.[32]

[32] Ann Simpkinson and Charles Simpkinson, *Soul Work: A Field Guide for Spiritual Seekers* (San Francisco: HarperCollins, 1998).

Practice patterns vary, but clients or patients are often seen for weekly sessions.

Formal counseling and psychotherapy approaches that are spiritually-oriented or spiritually-attuned are beginning to enter the mainstream of therapeutic practice. Although Jungian therapy and psychosynthesis had been articulated several decades ago, the number of such practitioners was rather small. Recently, significant developments in the theory and the clinical practice of Transpersonal Psychology, called Transpersonal Psychotherapy,[33] have occurred just as both clients and psychotherapists have been increasingly interested in integrating the spiritual dimension in their daily lives. Although referred to by varying designations, such as spiritual psychotherapy,[34] Christotherapy,[35] spiritual counseling and psychotherapy,[36] etc., spiritually-oriented psychotherapy approaches appear to be rather broad in focus. For example, transpersonal psychotherapy as described by Brant Cortright suggests that its focus is rather broad, encompassing Categories I, II, IV, and V. Moral guidance does not appear to have a place in this approach, although Cortright deals very directly with several ethical issues in the clinical practice of transpersonal psychotherapy. Roger Walsh, a leading proponent of transpersonal psychology and spiritually-oriented psychotherapy, contends that living ethically is a core spiritual practice across all the major world religious and spiritual systems.[37] Since spiritual practices are commonly incorporated in spiritually-oriented psychotherapies, it may well be that moral guidance

[33] Cortright, *Psychotherapy and Spirit.*

[34] T. Bryam Karasu, "Spiritual Psychotherapy," *American Journal of Psychotherapy* 53 (1999) 143–62.

[35] Bernard Tyrrell, *Christotherapy II: A New Horizon for Counselors, Spiritual Directors, and Seekers of Healing in Growth in Christ* (New York: Paulist Press, 1982).

[36] Len Sperry, "Spiritual Counseling and the Process of Conversion," *Journal of Christian Healing* 20:3 & 4 (1998) 37–54.

[37] Walsh, *Essential Spirituality.*

may become an additional focus of these approaches. Currently, it appears that only a few spiritually-oriented approaches include Category III issues as a focus.

The Need for Revisioning Pastoral Counseling and Spiritual Direction

Unfortunately, the current practice of spiritual direction and pastoral counseling is only partially responsive to the expectations of many directees and clients. A principal reason for this situation is reliance on reductionistic models and theories which emphasize one or two dimensions of human experience to the exclusion of the others. It may well be that uncritical over-reliance on psychological constructs and methods—at the expense of constructs and methods from moral theology, moral philosophy, cultural anthropology, and even biology—further fosters this reductionism and can unwittingly promote individualism and spiritual narcissism. Thus, it should not be too surprising that current approaches to training and supervision of pastoral counselors and spiritual directors are also likely to reflect reductionism and individualism. Accordingly, a more holistic and integrative model for the practice of spiritual direction and pastoral counseling is needed.

This book is an initial effort at revisioning the practice of spiritual direction and pastoral counseling. Revisioning is the process of critically reviewing a phenomenon, such as a theory or practice patterns. Distinct from a new vision which is an end point, such as proposing a new theory, revisioning is an intermediate activity. A basic contention of this book is that current theories are so theoretically reductionistic, individualistic, and clinically limited that efforts to establish a foundational theory are simply premature at this time. Nevertheless, it is both reasonable and possible to offer basic methodological guidelines and a conceptual map for framing a holistic and integrative model for the practice of spiritual direction and pastoral counseling.

Reductionism and Over-Reliance on Psychological Constructs

Reductionism involves analyzing constructs into simpler or lower-level constructs. "Reductionism is based on the view that there is a basic, single system of interrelations for all meanings, and that only when we come to this *one* substrate can we be said to explain fully the nature of some phenomenon."[38] For example, theorists may "reduce" constructs about behavior in psychology to biology and physiology on the assumption that physiological explanations are more rigorous and more likely to be quantifiable than psychological explanations, particularly depth psychology and psychodynamic theories of behavior that are "soft" and not easily quantifiable. Since constructs in pastoral counseling and spiritual direction (such as mystery, presence, discernment, and grace) are "softer" and less tangible than psychological constructs, it is not surprising that the disciplines of pastoral counseling and spiritual direction have come to favor psychological constructs over spiritual, moral, or religious constructs. Adopting such psychological reductionism has both benefits and costs. The main benefit is that both fields share a common language and set of constructs with the field of psychotherapy, which has increasing research support, clinical utility, and widespread acceptance. However, a major cost of such reductionism and uncritical over-reliance on psychological constructs is that only one or two domains of human experience are emphasized at the expense of the other domains.

Since the 1960s spiritual direction and pastoral counseling have readily imported various constructs and intervention methods from psychological theories. In some instances, entire theories have been adopted, albeit with minor modifications, such as Jung's theory of individuation,[39] Robert Assagioli's

[38] Joseph Rychlack, *A Philosophy of Science for Personality Theory* (Boston: Houghton Mifflin, 1968) 48.

[39] Carl Jung, *Psychology and Religion: East and West* (London: Routelage & Kegan Paul, 1958).

theory of psychosynthesis,[40] psychoanalytic theories (particularly object-relations theory and self-psychology),[41] and even Enneagram theory,[42] have greatly influenced how spiritual directors and pastoral counselors practice.

The Impact of Reductionism

During the past four decades, the impact of the psychological constructs and perspective on the way Westerners think about life has been enormous. Psychological constructs and explanations dominate our perceptions of reality. As a result, it is difficult to imagine spiritual matters without invoking psychological explanations. This has been called the "psychologization of spirituality."[43] Cortright provides a much needed reality test when he notes that "all the world's spiritual traditions arose from purely spiritual strivings and without access to the learnings of depth psychology."[44]

There are three stances with regard to the relationship of psychological and spiritual development. The first stance is that spiritual development is the same as psychological development, or the corollary, that spiritual development is a special form of psychological development. The second stance is the opposite of the first: spiritual development is separate and distinct from psychological development. The third stance is that psychological and spiritual development involve multiple, complex pathways that sometimes overlap and intermingle, and other times are separate.

Psychological experiences and development differ from spiritual experiences and development, and while they may

[40] Robert Assagioli, *Psychosynthesis: A Collection of Basic Writings* (New York: Viking Penguin, 1972).

[41] James Masterson, *The Real Self: A Developmental Self and Object Relations Approach* (New York: Brunner/Mazel, 1985).

[42] Don Riso and Russ Hudson, *Understanding the Enneagram,* rev. ed. (Boston: Houghton Mifflin, 2000).

[43] Cortright, *Psychotherapy and Spirit.*

[44] Ibid., 236.

overlap, the spiritual dimension is foundational and "achieving psychological integration is not essential for spiritual realization."[45] The first stance reflects the "psychologization of spirituality," while the second stance reflects denial. From the point of view of this thesis, both stances are untenable. The third is proposed as more consistent with Bernard Lonergan's theological anthropology[46] and more tenable as a foundational assumption for pastoral counseling and spiritual direction.

Another result of this reductionistic focus is the reluctance of therapists, spiritual directors, and pastoral counselors to deal with the moral concerns of clients. In the past the pastoral care and counseling function was typically provided by ordained ministers who would routinely deal with an individual's moral concerns. They offered moral guidance to individuals who were confused about moral choices or guided those who had violated established Christian norms through a process of forgiveness and restoration to the community. Practically speaking, there was no separation between pastoral counseling and ethics. Today, however, contemporary pastoral counselors, as well as secular psychotherapists, appear reluctant or unwilling to process moral and ethical issues with clients. This has resulted in a separation or split between pastoral counseling and the moral domain.

There are many reasons why pastoral counselors today are reluctant to deal with a client's moral and ethical issues. Prominent among these are a culture of pluralism and the pervasiveness of the psychodynamic perspective in pastoral counseling. In a pluralistic society ethical statements are more likely to be understood as personal opinions rather than as the consensus of a faith community. Poling notes that the "widespread acceptance of pluralism has effected dramatic changes in patterns of behavior found acceptable by the general population to whom pastoral care is directed."[47] Furthermore, the influence of psychoanalysis

[45] Ibid., 237.

[46] Bernard Lonergan, *Method in Theology* (New York: Herder & Herder, 1972) 78.

[47] Poling, "Ethical Reflection and Pastoral Care, Part II," 107.

and psychodynamic thinking has reshaped pastoral care and pastoral counseling from moral guidance into self-exploration and self-discovery. From the psychodynamic perspective, discussing ethical concerns in counseling were perceived as moralistic assaults to the embattled ego which fostered neuroses. The end result was that ethics became "reserved for preaching and teaching, . . . while pastoral care focuses on compassion and empathy to help individuals search their own experience, resolve their own conflicts, and decide their own norms."[48]

Since many individuals approach ministry personnel and pastoral counselors for help in deciding what is right, best, or appropriate for their lives,[49] the challenge is to balance moral guidance with compassion and empathy.[50] Browning notes that entering "into sensitive moral inquiry with troubled and confused individuals without becoming moralistic is the major technical and methodological task for training in pastoral care in the future."[51]

The situation is rather similar in spiritual direction. Prior to Vatican II, most spiritual direction in Roman Catholicism was provided by priests. Not surprisingly, spiritual direction took on a sacramental character and the discussion of one's daily life included not only prayer and spiritual practices but also moral matters, since the spiritual director was often a directee's confessor. One of the outgrowths of the Second Vatican Council is that spiritual direction is becoming increasingly the domain of non-ordained spiritual directors, and with it the functions of spiritual guidance and moral guidance have become separated. And, as spiritual direction became increasingly informed by psychology—particularly the psychodynamic perspective—rather than by moral theology, the split between spiritual direction and moral theology widened as it had in pastoral counseling.

[48] Ibid.

[49] Pruyser, *The Minister as Diagnostician.*

[50] Poling, "Ethical Reflection and Pastoral Care, Part II"; Browning, *The Moral Context of Pastoral Counseling.*

[51] Browning, *The Moral Context of Pastoral Counseling,* 3.

Commonalities between Spiritual Direction and Pastoral Counseling

As noted earlier, pastoral counseling and spiritual direction are typically considered to be separate and distinct entities. Training programs in pastoral care and counseling tend to be quite different than training programs in spiritual direction. Textbooks and core readings tend to be different. Their provision of care is different: pastoral counseling is associated with a pathology/crisis intervention model while spiritual direction is associated with a wellness/growth model. Furthermore, practice patterns, including renumeration, duration, and timing of sessions, are different. While pastoral counseling tends to be briefer in duration and to focus more on particular problems and concerns, spiritual direction tends to be longer-term and to focus more on ongoing personal growth and development. In other words, spiritual direction is not pastoral counseling.

Nevertheless, a relationship exists between spiritual direction and pastoral counseling. Both deal with an individual's life experiences. Both foster health, inner peace, resolution of a crisis or conflict, integration, as well as healing and wholeness. While pastoral counseling tends to focus more directly on the individual's relationship with a spouse, family members, or a peer, spiritual direction focuses more directly on the individual's encounter with God. Traditionally, spiritual direction has emphasized developing one's relationship with God which inevitably leads to greater integration of one's inner and outer life, while pastoral counseling emphasized integration of one's inner and outer life which could be expected to further develop one's relationship with God. Howard Clinebell was one of the first to observe that pastoral counseling had to be as concerned with spiritual growth as it was with the resolution of psychological issues.[52] He argued that pastoral counseling is most useful to

[52] Howard Clinebell, *Basic Types of Pastoral Care and Counseling*, rev. ed. (Nashville: Abingdon, 1984).

clients when it encompasses both the wellness/growth model as well as the pathology/crisis model.

In her book *Listening for the Soul: Pastoral Care and Spiritual Direction,* Jean Stairs describes the inevitable complementarities between pastoral care and spiritual direction.[53] Walter Conn, in *The Desiring Self: Rooting Pastoral Counseling and Spiritual Direction in Self-Transcendence,* also emphasizes the commonalities between the two disciplines in terms of goals and theoretical bases.[54] He notes that "the best of contemporary pastoral counseling includes the concerns of spiritual direction within it."[55] He contends that both pastoral counseling and spiritual direction share a similar goal: self-transcendence.

Reversing a historical trend of contrasting spiritual direction and pastoral counseling, these important books by Conn and Stairs suggest that the needs of spiritual seekers are more likely to be met if these commonalities are emphasized. *Transforming Self and Community* also assumes this basic commonality. Going beyond Conn and Stairs, it proposes a holistic, integrative model and then illustrates these commonalities in the actual practice of spiritual direction and pastoral counseling.

Concluding Note

Individualism and narcissism have become spirit-wounding forces in Western culture which have increasingly prompted individuals to find ways of incorporating spirituality in their daily lives. When their efforts are insufficient many seek spiritual direction and pastoral counseling. Unfortunately, current approaches to spiritual direction and pastoral counseling cannot fully meet the needs and expectations of these seekers. A major main reason for this shortcoming is that the

[53] Stairs, *Listening for the Soul.*

[54] Walter Conn, *The Desiring Self: Rooting Pastoral Counseling and Spiritual Direction in Self-Transcendence* (New York: Paulist Press, 1998).

[55] Ibid., 5.

theories underlying the practice of spiritual direction and pastoral counseling are reductionistic.

The corrective for limited and reductionistic theories would be a more holistic and integrative theory. Since the moral domain is notably absent from most psychological and spiritual theories and because clients often want help with moral as well as psychological and spiritual concerns, it would seem reasonable to integrate all three domains—moral, psychological, and spiritual—in future foundational models and theories. But, are such models and theories likely to be forthcoming? Fortunately, amidst the disappointment of such theoretical and practice limitations are some hopeful signs. Chapters 3–5 will describe the recent retrieval of the moral domain in both spirituality and psychology. Furthermore, researchers are heralding "positive psychology" and "positive social sciences"—the empirical study of human strengths and virtues—as the "Manhattan Project" for the social sciences in the twenty-first century. These are, indeed, promising developments that have the potential to significantly impact pastoral counseling and spiritual direction.

2

The Theoretical Bases for the Current Practice of Pastoral Counseling and Spiritual Direction

Reductionism is central to most current theories that underlie or inform the practice of spiritual direction and pastoral counseling. Ironically, these theories which portend to foster increased health and well-being seem to unwittingly foster and promote a culture of individualism and narcissism.[1] Two forms of reductionism were described in the previous chapter: domain reductionism and psychological reductionism. Both forms are evident in four prominent theories that underlie the practice of spiritual direction and pastoral counseling. The four theories are image of God theory, developmental stage theories, personality type theory, and self-transcendence theory. While each theory has considerable face validity which probably accounts for its popularity, few have any empirical validation, and all have significant limitations for the practice of spiritual direction and pastoral counseling.

[1] Ronald Rolheiser, *The Shattered Lantern: Rediscovering a Felt Presence of God* (New York: Crossroads, 1995); James Hillman and Michael Ventura, *We've Had a Hundred Years of Psychotherapy—and the World's Getting Worse* (San Francisco: HarperSanFrancisco, 1992).

Image of God Theory

Increasingly, clinical studies and survey research have elaborated image of God theory, which is also called *imago dei* and God-representations. Anna-Marie Rizzuto's classic clinical study of a series of patients as reported in the book *The Birth of the Living God* has sparked considerable interest among psychotherapists, pastoral counselors, and spiritual directors.[2] Rizzuto found that an individual's God-representation reflects one's images of parents or other early caretakers. Object relations theory is psychoanalytic perspective that informed her research on the formation of God representations.

Object relations theory takes its name from "object relations" or "object representations." Object relations signify the child's internalization of early significant individuals and the relational dynamics with such individuals, and the continuing psychic influence of these internalized object relations. Normally, object relations develop and mature over time. The three phases or processes of this development are symbiosis, separation-individuation, and object constancy. The basic development of one's God representation occurs during these phases, and specifically involves transitional objects.

Symbiosis is a development process wherein children come to experience a sense of themselves in relation to other persons. The children need caretakers, usually the parents, who from birth will provide a self-regulating or "holding environment" for them. A holding environment is the parents' capacity to communicate to children the message: "I'm strong enough to take care of you and protect you. I'm going to hold you. I'll take care of you. I'll comfort you. I'll soothe you." Things are perfect in the beginning, as the children's sense of self is merged with that of mother. The children most likely believe they are in control of everything, and they are as long as mom is at their beck and call.

[2] Ana-Maria Rizzuto, *The Birth of the Living God: A Psychoanalytic Study* (Chicago: University of Chicago Press, 1981).

Separation-individuation occurs throughout the course of life. The earliest occur when children gradually assume the holding and self-regulating function themselves. However, children are not ready to directly assume this responsibility, so they essentially "trick" themselves. It is as if the children say to themselves: "Let me take that holding function that's not under my control, but transfer it to an object, which is going to be much more clearly under my control." A blanket or teddy bear not only will be under the child's total control, but it soothes the anxiety of growing and becoming a separate person. There is a distortion of external reality, because the child treats the object with the properties that previously were shown to the child by the parent, the one who really had the soothing capacity. Transitional objects allow all of us to progressively exercise this holding/soothing function by proxy. Transitional objects help one in exploring one's environment and learning how to master it. It represents an intermediate step in the process of internalizing this self-regulating capacity. By age three or four children have developed enough capacity to understand and master the environment around them that they are now able reduce their distortion of reality.

A transitional object is an intermediate experience between self and object which serves to soothe separation anxiety and facilitate individuality, the sense of one's own unique identity. A related term is "transitional phenomena," which includes both transitional objects and "transitional modes." Transitional modes refer to later life experiences in normal persons. A transitional mode is a resting place or temporary suspension of higher ego functions like logical thinking which can free the person to deeply experience other modes of reality, such as music, the performing arts, or creative expression. In essence, the transitional mode has a soothing function, but for the purpose of further self-integration and self-transformation.

When speaking of God, the term "transitional object" is not used. This is because God is not an object, but rather a special type of object representation created by the child in that unique psychic space where transitional objects—whether toys, blankets, or mental representations—are provided with their powerfully real illusory lives. God is a transitional phenomena because God does not follow the usual course of other transitional objects. Generally, over the course of life the transitional object loses its meaning and value as the individual becomes a self-regulating person. On the other hand, instead of losing meaning God becomes more meaningful over the years. When other transitional objects can be repressed or even forgotten, God cannot be fully repressed. God is always potentially available for further love, acceptance, anger, or even rejection. God is psychically useful for us and remains a transitional phenomenon at the service of gaining leverage with oneself, with others, and with life itself. According to Rizzuto, God, like the teddy bear, has obtained half of his stuffing or holding function from his parents, and the other half of God's stuffing comes from the child's capacity to "create" a God according to his own needs.[3] This process of creating and finding God—this transitional phenomenon—never ceases in the course of life. It is further shaped and reinforced by culture. God has a special place in our culture such as in the dedication of our Constitution, our money system (coins & bills), holidays like Easter and Christmas, church buildings, tax credits, and the like.

Object constancy is the developmental process wherein children are able to enter into stable and loving relationships with others perceived as fully separate and independent from themselves—the children's image of God becomes less concrete and more conceptual. This cognitive development is facilitated, in large part, through fantasy. The earliest stage of fantasy is the imaginary companion. The imaginary friend or companion helps to solve daily problems in relating to others. Children's newly developing imaginations serve as a buffer in the harsh world they begin to experience. The imaginary com-

[3] Ibid., 179.

panion plays a specific positive role in child development, and once that role is fulfilled the "friend" tends to disappear. Specifically, the imaginary friend can serve as a scapegoat for badness or negative impulses, a playmate when no one else is available, a confirmer of the child's sense of omnipotent control, etc. The nature and structure of fantasy elaborates as children grow and develop. For male children, the sequence from three years onward is monster–devil–hero–super hero.[4]

Imaginary companions and monsters help children tolerate their badness, rageful impulses, deceptions, and frustrations. They also represent children's grandiose sense of power. It's been said that monsters help children know, master, and forget the monster children feel or fear themselves to be. At the age of two children learn that God is taken seriously by adults, that God will punish them, bless them, or love them. Though children can't see God, they come to sense that God is powerful, everywhere, and rules everything. Of necessity, children's God image utilizes the representation of the most significant parent available at the moment.

At two and one-half years of age children discover that things are made by people. They then question how things like clouds or oceans are made. Upon being told that God made them, children need to imagine that God is formidable enough to make big things like clouds. This kind of questioning and wonder continues through age five.

At age six children grasp the concept of God as creator of the world, of animals, and of beautiful things. And they begin to develop a feeling relationship with God. Prayer becomes important and they believe that prayer will be the answer. God's counterpart at this stage is the devil. It probably reflects children's hostile, sadistic parental representation. Later, as children begin to experience disillusionment with their parents, they are likely to have elaborate fantasies about having a set of ideal, imaginary parents, and fantasies of having a twin

[4] Ibid.

or a guardian angel to play with and guide them. Actually, it may be that Bible stories and pictures of heaven and a better life serve the same function as some of these fantasies.

Thus, by about the age of six a formal God representation is formed. Rizzuto notes that finally together with this colorful crowd of characters and amidst fantasies, wishes, fears, and sexual preoccupation, God formally arrives. God acquires a special and superior status because of multiple sociocultural religious, ritualistic, and family factors.[5] This representation continues to be modified and reinforced throughout latency and adolescence, particularly with images of heroes and super heroes: rock stars, sports figures, movie stars, and even politicians.

In summary, there appears to be a developmental sequence of the God representation: children grow and develop a transitional reality, an intermediate space, in which they can momentarily shift from being centered and dependent on their parents to the larger outside world. In early childhood children experience this transitional reality as one which is "alive" with imagined people and monsters. These images provoke intense feelings of fright and vulnerability that heretofore had been buffered by parents' deeply reassuring words and very presence. Often in this period God arrives on the scene of youngsters' consciousness. Because of what they have been taught by others, God becomes supreme, God is the ultimate: the strongest, the biggest, the best. As a result monsters now lose their terrifying power and grip over the children's imaginations. Later, the young children have internalized a simple cognitive notion of God which becomes part of how they see themselves in the world. As the children grow and begin the process of separating from their parents, they now can join the larger world. This process is facilitated because children have both an earthly father and a heavenly God with whom to relate.

If the developmental process proceeds normally, children learn to differentiate the earthly father from the heavenly father

[5] Ibid.

who is all-knowing, all-powerful, and all-protective. In this process of differentiation the earthly parent becomes less divine and more a fallible human being. In this critical time, the God image can become confused and distorted if differentiation is poorly accomplished. Distortions can also occur if the quality and consistency of children's bonding with their parents is compromised. The parents' own image of God also influences the formation of the young people's image of God. To the extent that the parental God image is relatively mature and that parent-adolescent relations are relatively harmonious, the adolescent is likely to have a realistic, balanced, and healthy God image. But to the extent that the parental God representation is distorted and parent-adolescent relations are ambivalent and conflicted, the young person is likely to develop a distorted representation and style of relating to God.[6] The quality of the relationship between parents cannot be overemphasized. Parenthetically, it has been suggested forming a God representation is somewhat different for young girls than it is for boys.[7]

Critique of Image of God Theory

Perhaps the major critique of God-representation and image of God theory is that there are no systematic empirical investigations published which validate the theory.[8] Nevertheless, there have been numerous doctoral dissertations on the topic and several survey studies reported. The survey research suggests some interesting correlations between God image and marital functioning, theological views, political party affiliation, and voting preferences.[9] From a holistic and integrative

[6] David Heinrichs, "Our Father Which Art in Heaven: Parataxic Distortions in the Image of God," *Journal of Psychology and Theology* 10 (1982) 127.

[7] David Heller, *The Children's God* (Chicago: University of Chicago Press, 1986).

[8] Kate Loewenthal, *The Psychology of Religion: A Short Introduction* (Oxford: One World Publications, 2000) 82.

[9] Wade Roof and Jennifer Roof, "Review of the Polls: Images of God Among Americans," *Journal for the Scientific Study of Religion* 23 (1984) 205.

perspective, image of God theory is rather limited in that it concerns only limited aspects of the spiritual and psychological domains while excluding the moral domain entirely.

Applications to Spiritual Direction and Pastoral Counseling

What is value and utility of God representations in pastoral counseling and spiritual development? Rizzuto describes the therapeutic value of understanding clients' God representations:

> Careful exploration of the subjective description of an individual's God may reveal precious information about the type of psychic and interpersonal events that led to the particular characteristics attributed to God. . . . An understanding of an individual's God representation may provide, in turn, information about his or her psychic history and the types of obstacles that interfere with potential belief, or with the updating of the God representation. I am referring now to [intrapsychic] processes . . . that may obstruct the transformation of the God representation and of religious behavior to a level more compatible with the individual's developmental moment.[10]

Leroy Howe, in the book *The Image of God: A Theology for Pastoral Care and Counseling,* describes an interesting clinical application of image of God theory.[11] He has correlated a theology of the image of God with object relations theory and applied it to the pastoral counseling setting. Similarly, Deborah Hunsinger, in her book *Theology and Pastoral Counseling,* has correlated Karl Barth's theology with the psychoanalytic perspective on God representations as the basis for practicing pastoral counseling.[12] Taylor reviewed Howe's *The Image of God* in

---

Andrew Greeley, *The Religious Imagination* (New York: William H. Sadler, 1981).

[10] Ana-Maria Rizzuto, "Religious Development: A Psychoanalytic Point of View," *New Directions for Child Development* (1991) 56–7.

[11] Leroy Howe, *The Image of God: A Theology for Pastoral Care and Counseling* (Nashville: Abingdon Press, 1995).

[12] Deborah Hunsinger, *Theology and Pastoral Counseling: A New Interdisciplinary Approach* (Grand Rapids, Mich.: Eerdmans, 1995).

an international journal for spiritual directors and found it to be directly applicable and useful to the practice of spiritual direction.[13] Both of these efforts have greatly extended this theory to clinical practice.

Regrettably, all these approaches focus only on the psychological and spiritual domains, and a very narrow psychological theory, psychoanalytic theory. Their emphasis is primarily on the affective dimension. Because they do not address the moral domain, nor other dimensions of human experience such as the intellectual, somatic, or sociopolitical, these approaches are somewhat reductionistic and also clinically limited.

Developmental Stage Theory

A number of developmental stage theories relevant to the spiritual domain were generated in the 1970s and 1980s. Among them were theories of moral development, faith development, self development, and spiritual development. Moral and faith development theories will be briefly described in this section along with a more detailed discussion of theories of self and spiritual development.

Moral Development Theory

Lawrence Kohlberg proposed a stage model of moral development which specifies three increasingly complex developmental levels involving six stages.[14] Kohlberg's intent was to describe the developmental process of moral reasoning rather than moral action, aware that the link between moral reasoning and action is elusive.

He proposed three levels of moral reasoning: pre-conventional, conventional, and post-conventional. He predicted that

[13] Sharon Taylor, "Review of *The Image of God* by Leroy Howe," *Presence: The Journal of Spiritual Directors International* 3 (1997) 73–5.

[14] Lawrence Kohlberg, *Essays on Moral Development* (New York: HarperCollins, 1984).

the relationship between moral reasoning and action would be strongest at the post-conventional level, where actions are theorized to be mediated by rational principles. The first developmental level, pre-conventional morality, is characterized by morality that is externally based and emphasizes external control. Stage 1 is the punishment and obedience orientation, while stage 2 is the instrumental relativist orientation wherein right and wrong are determined by what behavior gets rewarded. The second developmental level, conventional morality, is characterized by morality that emphasizes pleasing others or maintaining standards. Stage 3 is interpersonal concordance orientation, which is also called "Good boy," "nice girl" stage of moral development, while stage 4 involves social system maintenance, also called the law and order orientation. The third developmental level, post-conventional morality, involves moral reasoning based on abstract moral principles. Stage 5 is the social contract orientation, while stage 6 is the universal ethical principles orientation.

Faith Development Theory

Rather than conceptualizing faith in terms of specific beliefs, James Fowler conceptualizes faith as representing how individuals develop cognitively and spiritually in dealing with ultimate, transcendental reality and meaning.[15] He describes faith development in six stages, with a pre-faith stage representing an emergent stage in which a fund of trust and mutuality is built up during the first years of life.

Stage 1: This is called Intuitive-Projective Faith, which is a fantasy-filled, imitative phase in which children can be powerfully and permanently influenced by the visible faith of primary related adults.

[15] James Fowler, *Stages of Faith: The Psychology of Human Development and the Quest for Meaning* (San Francisco: HarperSanFrancisco, 1995).

Stage 2: This is called Mythic-Literal Faith, wherein individuals begin to take on for themselves the stories, beliefs, and observances that symbolize belonging to their community.

Stage 3: This is called Synthetic-Conventional Faith, where faith is structured in interpersonal but mostly conformist terms. This stage is normative for most adults.

Stage 4: This is called Individuative-Reflective Faith, in which the self and one's beliefs begin to take on a personalized system of explicit meanings to which one is personally committed.

Stage 5: This is called Conjunctive Faith, which involves the integration and syntheses of opposing ideas and beliefs. At this stage individuals have the capacity to critically analyze their beliefs and allow them to energize their behavior.

Stage 6: This is called Universalizing Faith, which involves looking beyond the constraining paradoxes and the specific content of one's particular faith to seek a future order of relating justly and lovingly to others.

Self-Development Theory

Robert Kegan has proposed a stage theory of self-development that is highly regarded by spiritual directors and pastoral counselors because it addresses the two basic human desires expressed in all spiritual literature: the desire for attachment or relationship, and the desire for separation or autonomy.[16] While this theory is less well known than either Kohlberg's or Fowler's developmental stage theories, this theory informs the practice of many spiritual directors and pastoral counselors. Accordingly, it is described in more detail than the other stage theories.

The basic dynamic of this model is that meaning-making is what defines human nature and that emotion is understood

[16] Robert Kegan, *The Evolving Self: Problem and Process in Human Development* (Cambridge, Mass.: Harvard University Press, 1983).

as the experience of defending, surrendering, and reconstructing a center of meaning. Self-other relations emerge from the ongoing process of development, which involve a succession of increasing differentiations of the self from the world. The result of this process is a more complex object of relation.

Basic to every stage of the development of the self is the continuous and evolving meaning-making evolution. Fusion, differentiation, and belonging are activities that recur in new forms at each phase of development as a person makes the meaning of "self" and "other" again and again. Each stage of development can surrender its controlling independence, for freely chosen interdependence involves balancing the universal longing for both autonomy and attachment. Unlike other stage theories, Kegan describes the necessity for development beyond the stage of autonomous self-direction, wherein control is favored over mutuality which inhibits intimacy. For Kegan, the most mature stage is one in which the self surrenders its controlling independence for freely chosen interdependence and relates to others with mutuality and equality. From this perspective, spiritual maturity becomes a matter of freely surrendering oneself and risking a genuinely mutual relationship with others and with God.

The specific stages of development are:

Stage 1: the Impulsive Stage, wherein the self evolves from the "Incorporative," which is undifferentiated and controlled by reflexes; Kegan labels it Stage "0." The impulsive self is embedded in and subjected to impulses and perceptions which are unorganized and constantly changing. The result is that the impulsive self can rapidly alternate between extremes of emotion. It cannot tolerate ambivalence.

Stage 2: the Imperial Stage, where in the emergence of concrete operational thinking children create an interior world and objectify impulses and perceptions. The result is that the self is no longer controlled by impulses and perceptions and can actively and purposefully explore its environment.

Stage 3: the Interpersonal Stage, wherein the self is able to relate to others by coordinating its needs with the needs of others and by exhibiting some measure of empathy.

Stage 4: the Institutional Stage, wherein a coherent sense of identity is achieved which means this self is able to separate itself from its relationships and can experience a sense of self ownership. At this stage this self is unable to fully and critically reflect on this organization.

Stage 5: the Inter-individual Stage, wherein the self becomes capable of surrendering its controlling autonomy and independence for freely chosen interdependence, and thereby relates to others with mutuality and equality.

Stages of Spiritual Development

David Helminiak has proposed a stage model of spiritual development.[17] His basic assumption is that spiritual development embraces all these dimensions of human development rather than being a separate line of development alongside physical, emotional, intellectual, moral, ego, or faith development. Spiritual development is a process of ongoing integration of the human spiritual principle into the deep structures of the personality, which is characterized by four factors: integrity or wholeness, openness, self-responsibility, and authentic self-transcendence. Helminiak describes five distinct developmental stages in this process of integration.

Stage 1: the Conformist Stage, which is the beginning point of spiritual development and is characterized by a deeply felt and extensively rationalized worldview, accepted on the basis of external authority and supported by approval of one's significant others.

Stage 2: the Impulsive Stage, which is characterized by beginning to assume responsibility for the awareness that because

[17] David Helminiak, *Spiritual Development: An Interdisciplinary Study* (Chicago: Loyola University Press, 1987).

of unthinking adherence to an inherited worldview one has actually abdicated responsibility for one's life. At this stage individuals begin to learn that their lives are what they decide to make of them.

Stage 3: the Conscientious Stage, which is the first true stage of spiritual development and is characterized by the achievement of significantly structuring their life according to their own understanding of things, by optimism regarding their newly accepted sense of responsibility for themselves and their world, and by commitment to their principles.

Stage 4: the Compassionate Stage, wherein individuals learn to surrender some of the world they have so painstakingly constructed for themselves. Their commitments are no less intense, but they are more realistic, more nuanced, and more supported by deeply felt and complex emotion.

Stage 5: the Cosmic Stage, in which as this final stage unfolds, an individual's habitual patterns of perception, cognition, interrelation, and all others become more fully authentic. There is a profound merging, insofar as it is possible, between spirit and self. It is that state of full integration and authenticity.

Critique of Developmental Stage Theories

To date, none of these basic developmental theories has held up well to the increasing scrutiny of theological critics and psychological researchers.[18] Both theoretical and praxis limitations have been noted. Prominent among these is reductionism. Furthermore, there is only marginal research support for the two most widely studied theories, those of Erik Erikson and Lawrence Kohlberg. Since these developmental theories or models principally address a single domain and one or

[18] William Spohn, "Spirituality and Ethics: Exploring the Connections," *Theological Studies* 58 (1997) 109–23; Owen Flanagan, *Self-Expression: Mind, Morals and the Meaning of Life* (New York: Oxford University Press, 1996).

two dimensions, while excluding consideration of the others, they are essentially reductionistic theories. Accordingly, they have limited value and utility as foundations for the practice of spiritual direction and pastoral counseling when viewed from the perspective of human experience.

Applications to Spiritual Direction and Pastoral Counseling

Joann Wolski Conn, in *Spirituality and Personal Maturity,*[19] and Elizabeth Liebert, in *Changing Life Patterns: Adult Development in Spiritual Direction,*[20] have utilized Kegan's model of self-development and skillfully articulated and demonstrated its clinical utility in spiritual direction and pastoral counseling.

Psychological Types Theory

The classification of human persons into types has a long history beginning with Hippocrates' humoral types. Today, there are two theories of personality types that are widely used by spiritual directors and pastoral counselors: the Enneagram and the Myers-Briggs Type Indicator (MBTI). Their popularity is related to the ease of helping others understand themselves and their relationships in terms of a limited number of personality types or categories: the Enneagram involves nine types while the Myers-Briggs involves up to sixteen types.

Both of these personality typing systems are based on different personality theories. The Myers-Briggs Type Indicator (MBTI) is based on Jung's theory of personality types or functions. The MBTI emphasizes the constructs of introversion/extroversion, sensation/intuition, thinking/feeling, and perceiving/judging. The Enneagram was initially believed to

[19] Joanne Wolski-Conn, *Spirituality and Personal Maturity* (New York: Paulist Press, 1989).

[20] Elizabeth Liebert, *Changing Life Patterns: Adult Development in Spiritual Direction,* rev. ed. (New York: Paulist Press, 2000).

have its roots in Sufi mysticism. However, recently Rohr and Ebert suggest the Enneagram has Christian earlier roots dating at least to the Desert Fathers.[21] In the theory underlying the Enneagram, each personality type is defined by a compulsion or basic driving forced to avoid unpleasantness. The basic compulsion is an individual's vice or "hidden sin" and "redemption" from one's compulsion comes from "moving against" that compulsion. Finally, both of these personality typing systems can be assessed through observation, interview, or psychometric inventories. Unlike the MBTI, which "began as a psychological inventory and was later employed in guiding spiritual development, the Enneagram began as the mapping of a spiritual practice that was psychologized when it was introduced into the West."[22] Since the Enneagram is more commonly utilized than the MBTI in spiritual direction, it will be briefly described in the following section.

Enneagram

The Enneagram is a system of human development which maps nine different personality types and their interrelationships. Each type differs in its world view and self-view. Each Enneagram type has a distinct set of talents and traps or compulsive strivings. Each has its own way of becoming imbalanced and its own way of achieving transcendence. Although every person could possess all the talents and traps of all nine patterns, each type characteristically engages in certain behaviors more than others. This pattern becomes a habitual or automatic way of being.

The Enneagram is an approach to personality typing that combines modern psychological understanding with ancient

[21] Richard Rohr and Andreas Ebert, *Enneagram: A Christian Perspective* (New York: Crossroads, 2001).

[22] James Empereur, "Personality Types," *The New Dictionary of Catholic Spirituality,* ed. Michael Downey (Collegeville: The Liturgical Press, 1993) 738.

teachings to provide a psychospiritual tool for personal development. Unlike most other systems and approaches, the Enneagram distinguishes one's personality from one's basic essence. The personality is that which appears as one's type traits and automatic, unconscious behaviors. It is akin to one's persona or "false self." On the other hand, essence transcends personality and reflects a universal quality and connects an individual with the spiritual domain. This is akin to one's "true" self. While the Enneagram system lends itself as a therapeutic tool in improving one's career and relationships, many therapists and spiritual directors view the Enneagram as a very powerful tool for spiritual development and transformation.

Two aspects of the Enneagram that spiritual directors find useful for spiritual development are the specification of virtues and vices for each type. The basic vices are akin to the seven capital sins of Christian tradition: pride, avarice, anger, envy, lust, gluttony, and sloth, to which are added fear and deceit. The virtues, then, are the polar opposites of these vices: humility, non-attachment, serenity, equanimity, innocence, sobriety or temperance, action, courage, and truthfulness.

The following are brief Enneagram descriptions of the nine personality types. Each characterization includes a description of the basic need and behavioral traits, as well as levels of functioning: healthy, average, and unhealthy. It also includes the basic virtue and vice associated with each type. These characterizations are based on the work of Don Riso and Russ Hudson[23] and Richard Rohr.[24]

Type 1 people have a need to be perfect. Thus, they strive to be right and avoid being wrong. They are often perfectionists and have a strong sense of morality. Healthy Ones exhibit conscientiousness, discernment, integrity, and strong sense of

[23] Don Riso and Russ Hudson, *Understanding the Enneagram: The Practical Guide to Personality Types,* rev. ed. (Boston: Houghton Mifflin, 2000) 66–135.

[24] Richard Rohr, *Discovering the Enneagram: An Ancient Tool for a New Spiritual Journey* (New York: Crossroads, 1993).

purpose in life. They live balanced, serene lives. Ones with an average level of psychological health and well-being are driven by an inner set of standards that tends to be quite rigorous, and independent of what other people might tell them. Hence, the average One is quite self-critical and critical of others when they expect the same high standards of others that they have imposed on themselves. Ones get much of their energy from anger; at best, this energy is channeled into discipline, organization, a strong work ethic, and a love of fairness, justice, and truth. Unhealthy Ones tend to be inflexible, opinionated, and trapped by their own rules and principles. Serenity is the virtue and anger is the vice associated with this type.

Type 2 people have a need to be needed. Thus, they focus their lives on giving and receiving love. They want to know that they are first in people's hearts, and enjoy the challenge of drawing people into their emotional web, often by seductive means. Healthy Twos are charming people who spontaneously help others, give thoughtful gifts, and make themselves indispensable without expecting anything in return. Average Twos still give to others, but may expect attention, material rewards, romantic favors, or other special privileges in return. They can be patronizing, overbearing, and even highhanded. They can play favorites and pretend to help others while creating dependency relationships that use others for their own emotional needs. Unhealthy Twos can be manipulative and self-serving in the quest to gain others' attention and favor. They feel entitled to get what they want and feel victimized if they don't get it. They then feel justified in using disparaging remarks, guilt, and even stalking to get what they want and need. Humility is the virtue and pride is the vice associated with this type.

Type 3 people have a need to succeed. They tend to be impressive individuals with impressive credentials and high profile friends and associates. They are adaptable individuals who are masters of managing the impression of being intelligent, talented, successful, and concerned about others. Accordingly, they easily win the admiration and trust of others, and tend to be sought out as public speakers and spokespersons for organizations and causes. Extroverted Threes tend to be charming and glib individuals who use their networking skills to enhance their image and careers, while introverted Threes are more likely to promote themselves through their skills and competence. Healthy Threes are authentic, self-accepting, inner-directed persons who can communicate with heartfelt simplicity and gentile graciousness. Average Threes tend to be driven individuals who are pragmatic, image-conscious, social climbing individuals who seek and expect recognition for their accomplishments and polished facade. Unhealthy Threes can be exploitative and deceptive, doing whatever it takes to succeed or convince others of their superiority. Truthfulness is the virtue and deceit is the vice associated with this type.

Type 4 people have a need to be special. They seldom settle for the ordinary and humdrum and are incredulous that most around them do. They combine emotional intensity with sensitivity and intuition. Extroverted fours have a deep need to express themselves in very personal ways, often with art, theater, or literature. Fours can be painfully self-aware people, which often motivates their interest in emotional and spiritual growth. Healthy Fours are emotionally honest and authentic. Because of their emotional awareness, fours can be extraordinarily compassionate and spiritually mature. Average Fours tend to bring this same emotional intensity to close relationships, often with dramatic and unsettling results. Unhealthy Fours tend to overly focus on and brood about their inner pain, which leads to despair or to becoming hyperactive and flamboyant to mask inner pain. Equanimity is the virtue and envy is the vice associated with this type.

Type 5 people have a need to perceive. Thus, the Five is the most mentally intense of all the types, but they tend to mask this intensity with an air of detachment. Fives tend to think before they act, just the opposite of most other types. Healthy Fives make excellent researchers, investigators, scholars, and scientists. They are highly independent and their need for privacy may lead to them becoming socially isolated, which can either lead to brilliance or weirdness, or both. Some Fives are intellectually arrogant, while others are very kind and thoughtful. Healthy Fives love learning, become experts in their field, and are highly imaginative and innovative individuals who are well grounded in life and have secure identities. Average Fives often have a cynical worldview and their tendency toward detachment makes their thinking quite idiosyncratic. Unhealthy Fives tend to be reclusive, eccentric, and suspicious individuals who can be quite antagonistic and emotionally overwrought. Nonattachment is the virtue and avarice is the vice associated with this type.

Type 6 people have a need for certainty and security. As such they tend to be affectionate while being careful and safety-minded. Female Sixes are likely to exhibit affection and appear dependent on others, while male Sixes are more likely to hide the degree to which they depend on others. Sixes are exquisitely sensitive to danger and so tend to seek the companionship of other like-minded individuals. While they can be endearing and playful, they are also anxious and reactive. Thus, they may simultaneously like others, but also fear the power that others have over them. They value trust, but may be afraid of trusting others who might hurt them. Sixes also have nostalgic tendencies and resist changes, which they find threatening. They may be afraid to take action on their own, and prefer to work in teams where a common goal and companionship permits them to feel protected. They tend to be unquestionably loyal to those whom they trust. Healthy Sixes are engaging, friendly, and playful individuals, albeit somewhat ingratiating. Average Sixes look to others for support and guidance and often seek reassurance since they are never quite sure that they are doing enough to be secure. Unhealthy Sixes may be clinging and self-disparaging to the point of experiencing phobias or panic attacks. Or, they may be present as counter phobic, i.e., acting tough and menacing while denying the need for support. Courage is the virtue and fear is the vice associated with this type.

Type 7 people have a need to avoid pain. Thus, they are fun-loving and adventurous individuals and so they tend to shun boredom and crave excitement. They are likely to be enthusiastic, naturally entertaining, and sometimes even sensationalistic. Sevens tend to talk fast, move fast, and are masters at multi-tasking. They are often the life of the party but will suddenly disappear when it's time to clean up. Healthy Sevens are exuberant and eternally youthful, while average Sevens are childish in their need for instant gratification. Healthy Sevens can be extremely productive while still having fun in their work. Unhealthy Sevens often battle against boredom, leading to breakdowns if boredom persists. Sobriety is the virtue and gluttony is the vice associated with this type.

Type 8 people have a need to be against. Eights are assertive, speak their minds, make quick decisions, and respect others who do the same. They resist working for others or being controlled by any authority, and often champion the underdog. They dislike threats to their dominance or individuals who hide information from them, and may force confrontations with others to elicit the truth. Eights crave being in control, but may also give autonomy to subordinates they trust. They may show a softer side and be unusually compassionate and understanding to those in need or trouble. However, Unhealthy Eights can be quite tyrannical, destructive, and self-serving. Healthy Eights are often very effective leaders, as are many ordinary individuals who are confident and refused to be used or dominated by others. Innocence is the virtue and lust is the vice associated with this type.

Type 9 people have a need to avoid. They give the appearance of being easy-going, patient, and pleasant individuals who are good listeners. While these traits are indeed present, most Nines experience considerable anxiety and anger that is hidden, even from themselves. Occasionally, this anger may erupt with an intensity that is often surprising to themselves and others. Average Nines typically have problems motivating themselves, and instead they "go with the flow" of the people around them. Healthy Nines are receptive, open, emotionally stable and unselfconscious. Unhealthy nines may be obstinate and stubborn and can be neglectful and irresponsible. Over time they become increasingly helpless and ineffectual. Action is the virtue and sloth is the vice associated with this type.

Critique of Personality Type Theories

There are four basic criticisms of such personality typing. The first criticism is spiritual and cultural in nature. Downey notes that the MBTI and Enneagram "categorize rich and diverse spiritual experiences far too neatly . . . [such that] serious reflection and discernment are avoided."[25] He also contends that personality typing systems like the Enneagram and the MBTI have "become virtual synonymous with spirituality in some circles. The result is that spirituality has become jargon-ridden. . . . It seems to have eclipsed the salvific as the governing category in spirituality."[26] The implication is that these approaches are reductionistic, in that the mysteries and language of Christianity are reduced to psychological categories.

A second criticism is philosophical. It is that personality typing is a violation of uniqueness and individuality; furthermore, the Enneagram's theory of three centers appears to deny the primacy of human free will. Using prefabricated categories for understanding and predicting human behavior is reductionistic and frustrates the self-understanding which these approaches propose to offer. Similarly, labeling oneself and others with these types can be demeaning.

A third criticism is scientific. While there is considerable face validity to both the Enneagram and the MBTI, there is considerably less research support for the validity of either approach. This is not to say there is no empirical support for

[25] Michael Downey, "Christian Spirituality: Changing Currents, Perspective, Challenges," *America* 170 (April 2, 1994) 8–12.

[26] Michael Downey, *Understanding Christian Spirituality* (New York: Paulist Press, 1997).

these approaches. Actually, when compared to image of God theories, self-transcendence theory, and of stage theories of self-development and spiritual development, the Enneagram and the MBTI have some empirical support, at least with regard to some of the paper and pencil inventories for assessing these factors. Psychometric data, i.e., validity and reliability data, has been reported on the *Stanford Enneagram Discovery Inventory and Guide*[27] and on the *Wagner Enneagram Personality Style Scales*[28] described in the paper and pencil inventories.

A fourth set of criticisms are theological and leveled primarily at the Enneagram. The basic strategy proposed for growth and change, "moving against" compulsion to find redemption, favors salvation-by-works and appears to exclude grace. Because the Enneagram is based on a theology of enlightenment and self-transformation, it appears to be incompatible with the Christian ideal of love and self-surrender, and the corollary of seeking both self and social transformation.[29] In short, like previously noted theories, personality type theories have been criticized as being reductionistic and self-focused. In addition, serious philosophical and theological reservations have been noted for the Enneagram.

Applications in Spiritual Direction and Pastoral Counseling

Several books applying Enneagram principles to spiritual development have been published in the past decade. These applications span the Judeo-Christian continuum. In the Catholic tradition these include Susan Zuercher's *Enneagram Companions: Growing in Relationships and Spiritual Direction.*[30]

[27] David Daniels and Virginia Price, *Essential Enneagram* (San Francisco: HarperSanFrancisco, 2000).

[28] Jerome Wagner, *Wagner Enneagram Personality Style Scales* (San Francisco: Western Psychological Services, 1999).

[29] Dorothy Ranaghan, *A Closer Look at the Enneagram* (South Bend, Ind.: Greenlawn Press, 1989) 32.

[30] Susan Zuercher, *Enneagram Companions: Growing in Relationships and Spiritual Direction* (Notre Dame, Ind.: Ave Maria Press, 1993).

In the Anglican tradition is Peter Ball's *Anglican Spiritual Direction.*[31] In the Jewish tradition is Howard Addison's *The Enneagram and Kabbalah: Reading Your Soul.*[32]

Self-Transcendence Theory

Walter Conn, in *The Desiring Self: Rooting Pastoral Counseling and Spiritual Direction in Self-Transcendence,*[33] has proposed a theory of self as the foundational basis for pastoral counseling and spiritual direction. He defines self-transcendence as the "radial desire of the self for both autonomy and relationship, the dual desire to be a self and to reach out beyond the self to world, others, and God."[34] It is a theory of a "dipolar self" in which there is a self-as-subject and self-as-object. This theory deftly integrates the seemingly contradictory themes of self-realization and self-surrender. Conn gives another name for this dual desire, "relational autonomy," and contends that the goal of both pastoral counseling and spiritual direction is to facilitate relational autonomy.

Critique of Self-Transcendence Theory

While this theory is possibly the best articulated foundational basis for pastoral counseling and spiritual direction, it is problematic because of its apparent reductionism. Conn's nearly exclusive focus on the spiritual and the psychological, i.e., affective and intellectual dimensions of human experience, effectively dismisses or subordinates the moral, somatic, and social dimensions. Furthermore, to assume that relational autonomy is the only goal of spiritual direction and pastoral counseling is similarly reductionistic. Finally, the major spirit-

[31] Peter Ball, *Anglican Spiritual Direction* (Cambridge, Mass.: Cowley, 1998).

[32] Howard Addison, *The Enneagram and Kabbalah: Reading Your Soul* (New York: Jewish Lights Publishing, 1998).

[33] Walter Conn, *The Desiring Self: Rooting Pastoral Counseling and Spiritual Direction in Self-Transcendence* (New York: Paulist Press, 1998).

[34] Ibid., 19.

ual and religious traditions emphasize transformation, not only of self but of the community, as the outcome of the spiritual journey rather than the much narrower primary focus on self and self-transcendence. Accordingly, transformation, rather than merely self-transcendence, is a more reasonable goal of spiritual direction and pastoral counseling. In addition, a more holistic formulation might be a tripolar self, in which "self-in-community" extends the dipolar self. Conn's theory specifies that two self-capacities, "autonomy" and "self-surrender," are essential for self-transcendence. By comparison, the integrative model proposed in this chapter posits thirteen requisite self-capacities as essential for transformation.

Applications in Spiritual Direction and Pastoral Counseling

A recent book on self-transcendence theory applied to spiritual direction and pastoral counseling is Conn's *Desiring Self: Rooting Pastoral Counseling and Spiritual Direction in Self-Transcendence.* While Conn provides a self-transcendence formulation of one case, there are no indications on how this formulation would be implemented in that case example or in others. Thus, at this time the clinical utility and practical applications of self-transcendence theory within spiritual direction and pastoral counseling that Conn promises in his book have yet to be demonstrated.

The Stages and Processes of Theory Development

A basic methodological issue that must be addressed in any serious discussion of pastoral counseling and spiritual direction involves the status of theory development in these two specialties. The mark of a discipline's maturity is reflected by the presence of validated theories. In the process of Western intellectual inquiry orderly stages of theory development can be described. The sequence of stages proceeds from observation to taxonomy to model and then to theory.[35]

[35] This discussion is based on the work of Talcott Parsons and Edward Shils, *Toward a General Theory of Action* (New York: Harper & Row, 1962)

A taxonomy is a formal way of classifying and ordering observations of a phenomena. For example, the dimensions of human experience represents a taxonomy. The listings and classification of symptomatic distress and impaired functioning for each diagnostic entities in DSM-IV is also an example of a taxonomy.[36] The value and viability of a taxonomy is determined by the extent to which it is comprehensive in ordering observation.

Models are simplified representations of a reality. They are means of specifying relationships between and among ordered observations—taxonomies—of ideas, concepts, or methods. The diagnostic system of DSM-IV is an example of a model of psychopathology. The value and viability of a model is determined by the extent to which it represents these relationships.

The next progression in the sequence is theory. Theory is defined as a means for explaining a wide set of observations and the relationships among these observations. The value and viability of a theory is determined by the adequacy of explanation. Unfortunately, there are few proposed theories that meet this test. For example, there are at least three hundred theories of psychotherapy, and each posits some explanation for how psychopathology originates and can be changed or cured. However, none of these theories has been scientifically validated. In fact, the DSM-IV is described as an a-theoretical model of psychopathology. It remains a model based on taxonomies since there is not sufficient understanding of the etiology and pathogenesis of mental disorders to fashion a viable explanatory account or theory of psychopathology. Although there has been considerable scientific progress in recent years, it is not anticipated that a viable theory of psychopathology will be forthcoming for quite some time.

It appears that in their enthusiasm to become professional specialties, pastoral counseling and spiritual direction have

---

50–1; and Chava Franfort-Nachmias and David Nachmias, *Research Methods in the Social Sciences,* 4th ed. (New York: St. Martin's Press, 1992) 38–40.

[36] The *Diagnostic and Statistical Manual, Fourth Edition* (DSM-IV) is the standard for diagnosing mental disorders in the United States.

short-circuited this sequence with disastrous results. The sequence was subverted by jumping from limited observation of human experience to positing models and theories or importing them from other disciplines. A major consequence of this short-circuiting is that current theories and models are notably reductionistic and have limited clinical utility and viability.

At this stage of their development and professionalization, it may be premature to expect that an adequate and viable foundational theory for the practice of pastoral counseling and spiritual direction will emerge soon. Rather, it is more realistic to focus efforts on the development of comprehensive and integrative taxonomies and models. To short-circuit this arduous and necessary stage in the sequence of theory development seems futile and self-defeating.

The integrative model detailed in Chapter 6 is not proposed as the definitive foundational model, but rather as an example of the direction model-building in pastoral counseling and spiritual direction might proceed. This proposed model integrates and correlates three taxonomies—of virtues, spiritual practices, and self-capacities—as they relate conceptually and practically to the dimensions of transformation.

Presumably, the outcome of this effort will have both positive and heuristic value. Its positive value would be evident to the extent that it improves the practice and outcomes of pastoral counseling and spiritual direction. Its heuristic value would be evident by proposed refinements to the model as well as the development of other integrative taxonomies and foundational models. Ultimately, such an integrative foundation will serve to bolster the identity of pastoral counseling and spiritual direction as separate from, albeit interdependent of, the psychological and human sciences, as well as to sharpen the focus of these areas of clinical practice.

Criteria for a Holistic and Integrative Model

Carolyn Gratton contends that those who practice spiritual direction and pastoral counseling are desperately "in need of an integrative theoretical framework as a foundation. . . . This framework would be multi-disciplinary, inclusive of the full spectrum of the dimension of the human person and of their life field."[37] Three key criteria are indicated by Gratton for such a theoretical framework. The framework must be integrative, multidisciplinary, and include the dimensions of human experience. Similarly, addressing the need for an integrative framework for pastoral counseling, Abigail Evans calls for the integration to include "spirituality and the ethical" in addition to the psychological dimension.[38]

An integrative model of pastoral counseling and spiritual direction that meets Gratton's three criteria will be described and illustrated. It is integrative in that it provides a critical correlation and synthesis of various psychological and theological constructs. It is multidisciplinary in that it draws upon the disciplines of spirituality, moral philosophy, systematic theology, moral theology, and personality theory and psychotherapy. In addition, it includes the psychological, spiritual, and moral domains of human experience. Finally, it emphasizes the process or journey of transformation and the dimensions of transformation. As such, it contrasts with the current reductionistic theories and models.

Conclusion

The chapter began with the context and current practice of pastoral counseling and spiritual direction beginning with human experience, i.e., client concerns and expectations. Next, it illustrated current practice with case studies of spiritual direction and pastoral counseling, highlighting not only theoretical, but also practical limitations of current practice. Four theories that are commonly utilized by spiritual directors and

[37] Carolyn Gratton, "The Ministry of Spiritual Guidance," *The Way Supplement* 91 (1998) 24.

[38] Abigail Evans, *The Healing Church: Practical Programs for Health Ministries* (New York: United Church Press, 1999) 127.

pastoral counselors were briefly described and critiqued: image of God, developmental stages, psychological types, and self-transcendence. Although favored by many, none has held up well to increasing scrutiny; there is only marginal research support for some aspects of each theory, and all have significant theoretical and praxis limitations, the most serious being reductionism as well as individualism. Consequently, it was concluded that they have limited conceptual viability, practical value, and utility as foundations for the practice of pastoral counseling and spiritual direction.

Rather than proposing a developmental stage approach, a construct such as image of God, a theory of self-transcendence, or any theoretical entity or approach, this book proposes a more holistic and integrative model. This integrative model both acknowledges the value of these previously described theories and models and incorporates elements from some of them. It includes all the domains of human experience.

3

Spiritual Perspectives on Transformation

The spiritual domain is integrally related to the psychological and moral domains as well as the meta-domain of transformation. The perspective one has about the spiritual journey and the dimensions of transformation influence one's view of spiritual direction and pastoral counseling. A broad understanding of the spiritual domain of life and its relationship to transformation is essential in the practice of spiritual direction and pastoral counseling. This chapter describes several aspects of the spiritual domain, including its relationship with the disciplines of spirituality and spiritual theology, the changing relationship of spirituality and moral theology, and its relationship to transformation. A significant portion of this chapter describes the importance of spiritual disciplines and spiritual practices and develops a taxonomy of spiritual practices.

The Spiritual Domain of Life

The spiritual domain includes all religious and spiritual experiences, feelings, thoughts, and beliefs about one's relationship to God and all that may transcend one's self. It involves one's beliefs and attitudes about the meaning of life, one's work, one's relationship, and resources such as talent, money, time, etc. Often synonymous with religion, this dimension also includes rituals, spiritual disciplines, and spiritual practices. Academically, the spiritual domain is associated with the disciplines of spiritual theology and spirituality.

Spiritual theology is the formal designation in Christianity for theological inquiry into the spiritual dimension. Historically, spiritual theology was subdivided into ascetical theology and mystical theology. Today, the designation "spirituality" appears to be the preferred term, and is commonly used as synonymous with spiritual, ascetical, and mystical theology.[1] This section describes the spirituality and its relationship with moral theology, the over-reliance of spirituality on psychological constructs, and spiritual disciplines and practices.

The Changing Relationship of Spirituality and Moral Theology

This section describes the changing relationship between the practice of spirituality and morality, which reflects the development of two related fields of theology and areas of pastoral ministry. It is derived from the writings of Mark O'Keefe,[2] William Spohn,[3] and Dennis Billy.[4] Billy and Donna Orsuto tersely summarize this relationship with a marriage metaphor: "the 'marriage, divorce and remarriage' of the Western Christian spiritual-moral tradition."[5]

An Old Testament passage provides a concise basis for a balanced spirituality and ethics: "This is what the Lord asks of you, only this: that you act justly, that you love tenderly, that

[1] William Spohn, "Spirituality and Ethics: Exploring the Connections," *Theological Studies* 58 (1997) 109.

[2] Mark O'Keefe, "Catholic Moral Theology and Christian Spirituality," *New Theology Review* 7:2 (1994) 60–73; Mark O'Keefe, *Becoming Good, Becoming Holy: On the Relationship of Christian Ethics and Spirituality* (New York: Paulist Press, 1995).

[3] Spohn, "Spirituality and Ethics," 110.

[4] Dennis Billy, "The Unfolding of a Tradition," *Spirituality and Morality: Integrating Prayer and Action,* ed. Dennis Billy and Donna Orsuto (New York: Paulist Press, 1996) 9–31.

[5] Billy and Orsuto, eds., *Spirituality and Morality,* 1.

you walk humbly with your God" (Mic 6:8). It is an inclusive, threefold challenge: (1) establish right relationships with God and others; (2) act with love and from the heart; and (3) form a spirit open to God's promptings. Furthermore, the Old Testament offers two role models of the combination of goodness and holiness. God and wisdom are designated as being both holy and good (Wis 7:22).

The Synoptic Gospels extend this sentiment. The call to discipleship (Mark 8:34) is similar to the all-inclusive challenge of Micah. The disciple who truly models Jesus attempts to integrate prayer and action, the spiritual and the moral life.

Likewise, in the Pauline texts, there is no separation between spiritual and moral strivings. The Christian life for Paul involves only one thing: "being in Christ" (1 Cor 1:30). It is a transformation in Christ with no separation between prayer and worship, on the one hand, and moral striving and virtue, on the other: "It is no longer I who live but Christ who lives in me" (Gal 2:20).

The Johannine literature highlights that love of God and the love of neighbor cannot be separated, implying a constant interplay between holiness and goodness. Thus, if one claims to love God but hates one's brother or sister, one is not being good or holy, but is rather living a lie (1 John 4:20). From the Johannine perspective, love of God must be grounded in a moral life of love of brother and sister.

Up until this point in history O'Keefe indicates that the "marriage" between spirituality and morality was strong and faithful.[6] However, the impact of Gnosticism, Montanism, and Arianism, as well as Augustine's Neoplatonic views, subtly began to separate goodness from holiness. Nevertheless, during the patristic era the inclusive call to holiness and goodness began to be understood in a new way, taking the form of the "Three Ways": the purgative way, the illuminative way, and the unitive way. In other words, becoming good and holy was seen as a de-

[6] O'Keefe, *Becoming Good, Becoming Holy.*

velopmental process involving a progression of increasingly integrated spiritual and moral growth in the Christian life.

A high point in the history of Christianity was the medieval era in which the unity of the spiritual domain and the moral domain achieved a new level of synthesis, particularly in the writings of Thomas Aquinas. This synthesis was most noteworthy in the second part of the *Summa Theologiae.* Here, Aquinas established that the Christian life becomes a unified moral and spiritual striving to attain the ultimate end of life: the beatific vision. The good and holy life was to be pursued by all Christians. It became understood as a life of virtue formed by charity and transformed by grace. In this understanding, charity became the central virtue. Aquinas continued the "Three Way" tradition, referring to it with the designations: beginners, proficients, and perfects.

In the era of the Counter-Reformation, a serious "separation" occurred between spirituality and moral theology, ultimately leading to divorce. These manuals of moral theology dominated moral thinking in the sixteenth and seventeenth centuries, although they originated during Aquinas's own lifetime. Notable was a shift in emphasis to human striving toward natural human ends rather than ultimate ends.[7] Accordingly, morality focused more on specific sinful acts that "opposed" specific virtues, rather than on overall character and the virtuous lifestyle. The "separation" or split between spiritual theology and moral theology became wider with each subsequent effort to clarify orthodox teaching. Moral theology also became increasingly estranged from systematic theology.

The Counter-Reformation era saw the birth of the spiritual classics written by the likes of John of the Cross, Ignatius of Loyola, and Teresa of Avila. A distinction between ascetical and mystical theology became tightly drawn in the eighteenth century. This distinction further "fragmented" the inclusive/universal call in terms of social class and culture. A two-tier

[7] Billy and Orsuto, eds., *Spirituality and Morality.*

perspective of Christian life inevitably emerged, and the "divorce" between moral theology and spirituality became complete. Although all Christians were expected to strive to be morally good, only a small, elite group (i.e., cloistered religious and contemplatives) were expected to strive to be holy. O'Keefe points out that while John of Cross resisted this view, most other spiritual writers advocated the split.[8]

The impact of the "divorce" between spirituality and moral theology was far reaching. As it lost its grounding in the moral and ethical realm, spirituality became increasingly elitist, otherworldly, individualistic, and detached from social justice. Not surprisingly, as it was no longer grounded in prayer and other spiritual practices, moral theology became increasingly abstract, more focused on unusual dilemmas, and subsequently more removed from everyday concerns of Christian living.

The pre–Vatican II era, from the time of Trent onward, continued these trends. Predictably, the tension between the spiritual and the moral domains remained strong. However, the time immediately before, during, and after Vatican II saw efforts to "reconcile" spirituality and moral theology. *Lumen Gentium* and other council documents advocated the "universal call to holiness" once again. Furthermore, as the Church began reclaiming the biblical and systematic roots of moral and spiritual theology, a "remarriage" between spirituality and moral theology became more likely. Developments in liberation and feminist theology as well as the influences of ecology and neo-Aristotelian ethics, including Christian virtue ethics, have furthered this reconciliation.

Re-Bridging Spirituality and Moral Theology

This section briefly indicates some initial efforts at reconciling or re-bridging the relationship between spirituality and moral theology. Billy and Orsuto capture the heart of the matter

[8] O'Keefe, "Catholic Moral Theology and Christian Spirituality."

in the title of their edited book: *Spirituality and Morality: Integrating Prayer and Action.*[9]

Brian Johnstone insists that spirituality and moral theology share a fundamental unity.[10] He indicates that

> spirituality considers the whole of theology and studies how it affects the believer's life of faith in community. Moral theology seeks to discover . . . the kinds of persons Christians are called to become and the norms that should guide their lives. Moral theology, therefore, is a more specific field within the broader "field-encompassing" range of spirituality.[11]

He adds that "spirituality and moral theology have a common goal. Both are ultimately directed to bringing persons into a transforming relationship with God in Jesus Christ. Thus, the disciplines are one in their starting point and one in their goal. They have, therefore, a fundamental unity." Nevertheless, there are differences between the two, particularly with regard to methodology, focus, concepts, and constructs.

While Johnstone[12] believes that there are some promising connections between spirituality and ethics, Spohn[13] argues that there are also problematic connections, and these should not be dismissed easily. Nevertheless, he points to some commonality with regard to concepts and constructs. For instance, he notes that "perception, motivation, and identity are three regions of moral experience where the concerns of spirituality are supplementing, if not supplanting, formal ethical approaches."[14] More specifically he explains that, of these three concepts, "ethics and spirituality make identity a central concern."[15]

[9] Billy and Orsuto, eds., *Spirituality and Morality.*

[10] Brian Johnstone, "The Dynamics of Conversion," *Spirituality and Morality,* ed. Billy and Orsuto, 32–48.

[11] Ibid., 45.

[12] Ibid.

[13] Spohn, "Spirituality and Ethics," 109.

[14] Ibid., 114.

[15] Ibid., 119.

Johnstone further contends that "spirituality and morality come together in the original experience of conversion."[16] Similarly, O'Keefe asserts that spirituality and ethics intersect in the context of religious conversion:

> The moral and spiritual efforts of Christians, then, are distinct but inseparable aspects of their continual conversion. The effort to become morally good and to perform right actions, together with the effort to grow in authentic relationships with God and others, nurture and support—in fact, constitute—the ongoing conversion of Christians.[17]

A Taxonomy of Spiritual Practices

Distinguished transpersonal psychiatrist and philosopher Roger Walsh describes seven central spiritual practices in his book *Essential Spirituality: The Seven Central Practices to Awaken Heart and Mind.*[18] He indicates that while there are many spiritual practices, the seven he describes are consistent with the "perennial philosophy"—the view that there are common beliefs and themes shared by all the great world religions—and can therefore be called "perennial practices."[19] These seven central practices are: purify motivation, cultivate emotional wisdom, live ethically, develop a peaceful mind, cultivate wisdom and spiritual intelligence, recognize the sacred in all, and engage in the services of others. In the foreword to Walsh's book, the Dalai Lama of Tibet suggests that all seven practices are essentially linked to the development and practice of the virtue of compassion.

Walsh distinguishes spiritual practices from spiritual techniques and exercises. He uses the term "practice" to refer to the disciplines of developing crucial capacities of the heart and

[16] Ibid., 126.

[17] O'Keefe, *Becoming Good, Becoming Holy,* 42.

[18] Roger Walsh, *Essential Spirituality* (New York: J. Wiley, 1999).

[19] Ibid., 9–10.

mind, while the terms "technique" and "exercise" refer to specific methods for achieving a spiritual practice. For instance, the techniques of meditation and centering prayer are highly effective in achieving the practice of developing a peaceful mind. Some techniques can be useful in achieving two or more spiritual practices; for example, meditation is also a useful method for cultivating wisdom and spiritual intelligence.

Interestingly, Walsh indicates that these various practices are interrelated and suggests a developmental sequence to them. For example, he indicates that developing a peaceful mind, spiritual practice four, is facilitated by cultivating the first three spiritual practices. Each of these seven spiritual practices will be briefly discussed, and subsequent sections of this chapter will describe and illustrate some common techniques or methods.

Purifying Motivation

The purpose of this spiritual practice is to reduce one's cravings and redirect one's motivations or desires. For most individuals, this means relinquishing attachments to beliefs, feelings, possessions, and the desire for possessions or experiences or vices that impede them in their quest for true happiness. In so doing persons become better able to transform their motivations by reducing cravings, thus finding their soul's basic desire or higher motives, which Walsh indicates is a central goal of all spiritual practices. He notes that at the peak of higher motives is the pull to self-transcendence, which is defined as "the desire to transcend our usual false, constricted identity, to awaken to the fullness of our being, and to recognize our true nature and our relationship with the sacred."[20]

Cultivating Emotional Wisdom

Since emotions can dominate a seeker's life, transforming one's emotions is an essential spiritual practice. The great reli-

[20] Ibid., 53.

gious and spiritual traditions indicate three ways in which this occurs: (1) by mastering and reducing toxic and painful affects such as fear and anger; (2) by fostering positive attitudes such as gratitude and generosity; and (3) by cultivating such positive emotions as love and compassion. The goal is neither indulgence nor repression of emotions, but rather appropriateness, balance, and equanimity; in other words, the capacity to experience the inevitability of the ups and downs of life without becoming victim to mood lability. Learning how to release, transform, and appropriately use emotions is the basis of emotional wisdom.

Living Ethically

Walsh contends that "ethical living is one of the most powerful yet misunderstood of all religious practices."[21] However, when it is correctly understood and practiced it is an essential means for spiritual growth, and without it progress is difficult. Unethical acts "create deep deposits of fear and guilt, paranoia and defensiveness, . . . agitate and cloud our minds, making it difficult to achieve calm and clarity."[22] Unethical living is destructive to both self and others, and has immediate and long-term consequences: we become what we do and how we act. To live ethically involves practicing right speech and right action. It also involves dealing with the emotional residue remaining from past unethical behavior; in other words, making restitution and dealing with guilt feelings.

Developing a Peaceful Mind

As individuals are less compelled by craving and compulsive need, less troubled by painful affects, and less disturbed by ethical lapses, they become better disposed to concentrate and focus their attention, resulting in sense of calm and inner

[21] Ibid., 117.
[22] Ibid., 121.

peace. "This peace is the doorway to the sacred, when the mind is focused and unperturbed, it opens effortlessly to its Source."[23] The challenge of mastering this sense of attention and inner peace is a slow process aided by such methods as meditation, contemplation, yoga, and continuous prayer. It also involves transforming the complexity and clutter of everyday life and, as much as possible, transforming daily activities into sacred rituals and moments of awareness. Needless to say, it requires the regular and habitual use of various meditative and focusing methods.

Recognizing the Sacred in All

"Awakening sacred vision" is another term for discerning or seeing the sacred in all persons, things, and situations. This is a principal focus of spiritual direction in the Christian tradition, as it is in other religious systems that advocate formal spiritual direction or spiritual guidance. "What we perceive is selected by our desires, colored by our emotions, and fragmented by our wandering attention. What we see outside us reflects what is inside us. The result: we do not see ourselves or the world clearly or accurately."[24] Walsh contends that living mindlessly exacts a significant toll physically, emotionally and spiritually, and unhealthy cravings, motives, and emotions are most likely to surface during these moments of mindlessness. The corrective is mindfulness. "To love mindfully is to bring greater awareness to each activity, to be more present in each moment, and to catch subtle experiences that all too often go unnoticed."[25] Mindfulness not only enhances our awareness of relationships and the world within and around us, it also frees us from "automaticity," the sense of being locked on mental autopilot. With regular practice of mindfulness, these "initial glimpses gradually become a recurrent vision, peak experiences

[23] Ibid., 168.
[24] Ibid., 175.
[25] Ibid., 177.

extend into plateau experiences, altered states of consciousness became altered traits of consciousness."[26]

Cultivating Wisdom and Spiritual Intelligence

Walsh defines wisdom and spiritual intelligence as "deep understanding and practical skill in the central issues of life, especially existential and spiritual issues."[27] The quest for wisdom includes finding meaning and purpose in life, managing relationships and aloneness, living in the face of mystery, coping with illness, suffering, and death, and knowing and truly accepting oneself. The wise person is one who has developed deep insight into these issues as well as skills for dealing with them. Wisdom is a liberating spiritual capacity. It can dissolve one's delusions about self, just as it can reduce one's suffering and speed the awakening of one's heart and mind. Finally, by "loosening the bonds of egoism, wisdom also fosters concern and compassion for others."[28]

Engaging in the Service of Others

Altruism or helping others is viewed by the great religions as a central human desire, and recent psychological research seems to confirm that individuals are altruistic by nature.[29] "So esteemed are generosity and service that some traditions regard them as the essence of spiritual life, the practice upon which all other practices converge. . . . The supreme goal of enlightenment is sought, not for oneself alone, but to better serve and enlighten others."[30] Thus, as spiritual seekers become increasingly enlightened it is to be expected they will become

[26] Ibid., 206.

[27] Ibid., 216.

[28] Ibid., 248.

[29] Samuel Oliner and Pearl Oliner, *The Altruistic Personality* (New York: Free Press, 1988).

[30] Walsh, *Essential Spirituality*, 256.

sages, sages who dedicate themselves to the welfare of others and of life. Walsh notes that the first six spiritual practices lay the groundwork for generosity. Nevertheless, he describes several specific methods and techniques for cultivating generosity directly. This spiritual practice has the advantage of transforming all of one's daily activities into spiritual practices. "With its help we need not change what we are doing so much as how and why we are doing it. . . . With this approach, work life, and each project or family activity can be transformed into a sacred act."[31]

Concluding Note

This chapter discussed several aspects of the spiritual domain, including its relationship with the disciplines of spirituality and spiritual theology, the changing relationship of spirituality and moral theology. Historically, holiness was the defining characteristic of spiritual theology, while goodness was the defining characteristic of moral theology. Now, as then, transformation is meant to be both good and holy. There has been a complex relationship between Christian spirituality and moral theology, which has become quite strained over the centuries. Nevertheless, both are ultimately directed to fostering a transforming relationship between a person and God in Jesus Christ. A taxonomy of seven classes of spiritual practices was described. This taxonomy is a significant component of the holistic, integrative model of spiritual direction and pastoral counseling which is presented in Chapter 6.

[31] Ibid., 266.

4

Moral Perspectives on Transformation

The moral domain is integrally related to the psychological and spiritual domains as well as the meta-domain of transformation. It was previously noted that because of the reductionism of most theories of spiritual direction and pastoral counseling, there has been little or no place for the moral domain in psychotherapy, spiritual direction, and pastoral counseling, except for professional ethic codes. The specialty of philosophical counseling has emerged in response to this reductionism. Interestingly, at the same time pastoral counseling and spiritual direction seem to be ignoring the moral domain, interest in morality and character among the public is extraordinarily high, as is the renewed interest in morality, virtue ethics, and the empirical study of virtues among academics and researchers.

This chapter begins with a description of the moral dimension of life and focuses on character and virtue. The relationship of character and virtue and the recent retrieval of the character/virtue tradition in both moral philosophy and theology as well as in experimental psychology is described. It discusses various efforts to classify virtues over the years. Much of the chapter is devoted to describing a taxonomy of virtues applicable to the practice of spiritual direction and pastoral counseling.

The Moral Domain of Life

The moral domain refers to ethical thinking, decision making, and actions involving all the relationships in one's life: self, interpersonal, work, family, community, and peers. Commitment and social involvement, which includes attendance at religious or spiritual services and activities, tends to have a prophylactic effect on health and well-being. Individuals who engage in spiritual practices such as prayer, meditation, reading sacred writings, and seeking spiritual counsel and support from religious leaders and community during stressful times tend to adjust better to crises and problems. Religious commitment is usually associated with a decreased likelihood of experience depression. Attendance at religious services is related to marital satisfaction and adjustment, less divorce, less use or abuse of alcohol or drugs, lower rates of premarital sex, teenage pregnancy, and delinquency. Finally, there is less clinical depression among the elderly.

The Retrieval of Character and Virtue in Moral Theology

A Christian is one who accepts the call to discipleship and whose life is shaped by that call. This process is called conversion or transformation. Jesus' call (Mark 1:15) is a call to repentance, to a change of mind and heart, and to a new mode or style of living in keeping with that change. It requires a change in one's identity and basic orientation toward life. In other words, the call to Christian conversion is a call to become a person of good character. Accordingly, a person of good character is one who is engaged in the process of conversion, and so takes responsibility for his or her actions and has the capacity for healthy, life-giving relationships.[1]

Traditionally, moral theology has emphasized the concept of character, defining moral character as "that which gives orientation, direction and shape to our lives."[2] Moral character is related to two other concepts: habit and virtue. Habits are regular patterns of activity; virtues are perfected, rightly ordered habits, while vices are perfected, wrongly ordered habits.

[1] Donald Gelpi, *The Conversion Experience: A Reflective Guide for RCIA Participants and Others* (New York: Paulist Press, 1998).

[2] Richard McBrien, *Catholicism,* new ed. (San Francisco: HarperSanFrancisco, 1994) 1235.

> Character emerges from the network of virtues (or vices) . . . . Character, like conversion, can never be finished once and for all. A pattern of habits can be reversed or broken. Sometimes conversion occurs gradually; at other times it may occur through a single decisive act (as in a profound conversion experience, or in mortal sin).[3]

Similarly, Stanley Hauerwas notes that virtue and character require effort on the part of the individual.[4]

Is moral character the same as psychological character? Moral character can be differentiated from psychological character and personality traits as well as from temperament. Moral character involves the "sum and range of specifically moral qualities or traits the individual or community possesses, . . . a particular class of distinctive traits embedded within the wide matrix of traits comprising an individual's full descriptive character."[5] Hauerwas[6] carefully distinguishes the moral philosophical designation of character from the traditional psychological designation of character, personality traits, and temperament, particularly as described in popular books by Wilhelm Reich[7] and Rudolph Allers.[8]

> For the idea of character in its most paradigmatic usage indicates what a man can decide to be as opposed to what a man is naturally. . . . Therefore, if we know a man's character we think we have some indication about the kind of actions in which he is likely to engage.[9]

[3] Ibid., 926.

[4] Stanley Hauerwas, *Character and the Christian Life: A Study in Theological Ethics* (Notre Dame, Ind.: University of Notre Dame Press, 1975).

[5] William Brown, *Character in Crisis: A Fresh Approach to the Wisdom Literature of the Old Testament* (Grand Rapids, Mich.: Eerdmans, 1996) 7.

[6] Hauerwas, *Character and the Christian Life.*

[7] Wilhelm Reich, *Character Analysis* (New York: Noonday Press, 1966).

[8] Rudolph Allers, *The Psychology of Character* (New York: Sheed & Ward, 1931).

[9] Hauerwas, *Character and the Christian Life,* 12–13.

Unlike character, which involves decision making, for Hauerwas temperament is what a person is naturally and is embodied in the kind of character a person manifests.

In popular parlance character and virtue are often used interchangeably, but in moral theology and moral philosophy they are usually differentiated. Character refers to a unified, fundamental orientation of the self. It is the cluster of virtues which makes an individual what he or she is. Virtue, on the other hand, is the disposition or attitude that moves an individual to sustain practices, which enables the agent to accomplish moral good.[10] Virtues are powers that enable one to establish and nurture life-giving and healthy relationships. They prompt one to act but in such a way as to exclude extreme actions, i.e., the virtue of hope which is situated between the extremes of presumption and despair. Similarly, Hauerwas distinguishes character from virtue. Character is understood as a "more general orientation to life than virtue but that having character is a more basic moral determination of the self. The various virtues receive their particular form through the agent's character."[11]

The Retrieval of Character and Virtue in Psychology

Why is the moral dimension in psychology and psychotherapy described as the "neglected" dimension? A brief review of the history of psychology and psychotherapy provides an answer. As psychology evolved as a discipline and field of inquiry, it attempted to distinguish itself from its roots in moral philosophy. While a particular moral philosophy emphasized the common good, values and virtue, rational judgment, and will or the volitional aspects of character, psychology increasingly focused on individuality, behavior, emo-

[10] Alasdair MacIntyre, *After Virtue,* 2d ed. (Notre Dame, Ind.: University of Notre Dame Press, 1984).

[11] Hauerwas, *Character and the Christian Life,* 16.

tion and non-rationality, value-neutrality, and the unconscious aspects of personality.

The most effective strategy psychology utilized for both distinguishing and distancing itself from its roots in the field of philosophy was by differentiating the study of personality from the study of character. Gordon Allport was one of many academic psychologists to banish the notion of character from American psychology. His famous dictum—"Character is personality evaluated, and personality is character devalued"[12]—suggests psychology's disdain for the concept of character.

As a result of this focus, psychology succeeded in establishing a scientific and, presumably, a value-free foundation distinct from a philosophical foundation for understanding human behavior and actions. For all practical purposes, the concept of character in the field of psychology, once a commonly studied phenomenon, has been almost entirely replaced with the concept of personality.[13]

From the late 1950s through the early 1970s the profession of psychology endeavored to reformulate psychotherapy into the same scientific, value-free discipline framework as the rest of psychology. Unfortunately, many psychotherapists have become increasingly dissatisfied with this supposedly value-free, scientific view of psychotherapy as represented by DSM-IV, clinical practice guidelines, and treatment outcome measures. Critiques of psychotherapy's value-free stance are long standing. They include Philip Rieff's provocative analysis in *Freud: The Mind of a Moralist and Triumph of the Therapeutic*,[14] as well as Jerome Frank's *Psychotherapy and the Human Predicament*.[15]

[12] Gordon Allport, *Personality: A Psychological Interpretation* (New York: Holt, 1937) 252, emphasis added.

[13] Charles Taylor, *Philosophical Arguments* (Cambridge, Mass.: Harvard University Press, 1995).

[14] Phillip Rieff, *The Triumph of the Therapeutic* (New York: HarperCollins, 1966); Phillip Rieff, *Freud: The Mind of a Moralist* (Chicago: University of Chicago Press, 1959).

[15] Jerome Frank, *Psychotherapy and the Human Predicament* (New York: Shocken, 1978).

Frank observes that all psychotherapies share a value system which accords primacy to self-fulfillment and views individuals as the center of their moral universe. He believes that this value system can easily become a source of misery in itself because of its unrealistic expectations for personal happiness and because it downplays traditional values such as "the redemptive power of suffering, acceptance of one's lot in life, adherence to tradition, self-restraint and moderation."[16]

More recently, Philip Cushman suggests that the goal of attaining and maintaining an "autonomous self" may be misguided.[17] Furthermore, Cushman contends that such a preoccupation with an inner-self that is self-soothing, self-loving, and self-sufficient eventually leads to an "empty self."[18]

In addition, there is mounting concern that traditionally practiced psychotherapy tends to foster individual self-fulfillment over community well-being. For example, in *We've Had a Hundred Years of Psychotherapy and the World's Getting Worse,* James Hillman and Michael Ventura contend that psychotherapy has been so successful that it has effectively refocused our view of the problems of daily life into personal issues and reframed our view of the communal world in terms of psychopathology.[19] They note that therapy tends to draw sensitive, intelligent people away from the political arena into introspection and support groups. The result is that any motivation these individuals might have had to improve their local community, such as helping hungry, illiterate, or homeless people, is effectively displaced. Furthermore, they note that

[16] Ibid., 6–7.

[17] Philip Cushman, "Why the Self Is Empty," *American Psychologist* 45 (1990) 599–611; Philip Cushman, *Constructing the Self, Constructing America: A Cultural History of Psychotherapy* (Reading, Mass.: Addison-Wesley, 1995).

[18] Cushman, *Why the Self Is Empty.*

[19] James Hillman and Michael Ventura, *We've Had a Hundred Years of Psychotherapy—and the World's Getting Worse* (San Francisco: HarperSanFrancisco, 1992).

most therapeutic approaches have little to say about character, conscience, or commitment. In others words, psychotherapy has effectively changed the view of morality from a social ethic to an individual ethic.[20]

Some researchers and clinicians are proposing that values and ethics can and must be integrated into a scientific understanding of psychology and psychotherapy. Rather than being viewed as "getting in the way" of a science and practice of psychotherapy, values and ethics should be recognized as integral to any science that claims to systematically study the human person. This view offers a compelling way to re-conceptualize psychotherapy that retains many of its foundations while challenging it to greater social relevance and responsibility. It acknowledges that psychology and psychotherapy are value-laden enterprises, and it requires that mental health professionals consciously integrate values, morality, ethics, and politics into their professional efforts. The result will be a science that better reflects the fullness of human life, that is more effective in practice, and that, as a result, promises more fulfillment to psychotherapists.

Does the practice of psychotherapy make a significant and positive contribution to human welfare and the struggle for a good society? In *Re-envisioning Psychology: Moral Dimensions of Theory and Practice,* Frank Richardson, Blaine Fowers, and Charles Guignon present a reinvigorating look at psychology and psychotherapy and their societal purpose, and offer an alternative philosophical foundation, hermeneutics, from which psychotherapists can more incisively examine their work.[21] They issue a call for a new perspective on the societal value of psychology and psychotherapy and aim to reinvigorate individual psychotherapists' belief in the larger purposes of their own work.

[20] Frank Richardson, Blaine Fowers, and Charles Guignon, *Re-envisioning Psychology: Moral Dimensions of Theory and Practice* (San Francisco: Jossey-Bass, 1999).

[21] Ibid.

Efforts to Classify Virtues

Aristotle was one of the first to propose a classification schema or taxonomy of virtues. His original classification presented in *Nicomachean Ethics* included at least eleven moral virtues.[22] Four "cardinal virtues"—prudence, justice, temperance, and courage—were re-affirmed and appropriated from the Aristotelian tradition to Christianity by Thomas Aquinas. To these four Aquinas added three theological virtues: faith, hope, and charity, which find support in the New Testament. Recently, James Keenan has argued that there are really only two cardinal virtues: temperance and courage, which serve to support the virtue of justice, for which prudence simply specifies the situation and circumstances for acting justly.[23] Accordingly, Keenan has made the case for revising the notion of the cardinal virtues to include four basic virtues: prudence, justice, fidelity, and self-esteem or self-care, with two supporting virtues: temperance and courage.[24] His rationale is rather simple and integrated. Keenan argues that while justice calls us to regard everyone equally, fidelity calls us to pay special attention to family and friends, and self-esteem calls us to take care of ourselves. Keenan has recently designated self-esteem as "self-care."[25] These three claims are made simultaneously and it is the virtue of prudence that helps us discern which of the three to attend to at any given moment.

The cardinal virtues are acquired virtues which have a purpose directed toward right actions. The cardinal virtues are related to but different from the theological virtues of faith, hope, and charity, in that the theological virtues are directed to God rather than right action. Aquinas described the theologi-

[22] Benjamin Farley, *In Praise of Virtue: An Exploration of the Biblical Virtues in a Christian Context* (Grand Rapids, Mich.: Eerdmans, 1995).

[23] James Keenan, "Proposing Cardinal Virtues," *Theological Studies* 56:4 (1995) 709–29.

[24] Ibid.; James Keenan, *Virtues for Ordinary Christians* (Kansas City, Mo.: Sheed & Ward, 1996).

[25] Keenan, *Virtues for Ordinary Christians.*

cal virtues as infused virtues—in contrast to the cardinal virtues—which cannot be acquired or learned since they are God's gift to us.[26]

To date there have been few, if any, efforts to classify virtues, much less to consider the place of virtue in the context of pastoral counseling and spiritual direction. This book proposes that virtue should permeate all aspects of pastoral counseling and spiritual direction, including the goal of fostering virtues in clients and directees as well as in pastoral counselors and spiritual directors. The result would be virtuous clients and directees as well as virtuous pastoral counselors and spiritual directors. Virtue is fostered in clients and directees not only through the counselors' and directors' exhortation to practice virtue, but through the virtuousness of the exhorters themselves.

There is growing awareness that helping professionals, including pastoral counselors and spiritual directors, are expected to be virtuous persons.[27] For example, in his book on ethical aspects of pastoral ministry, Richard Gula contends that the "community of faith assumes that whoever takes on the role of minister is a virtuous person called to exercise virtue in the practice of ministry."[28]

So what virtues characterize the virtuous pastoral counselors and spiritual directors? To date, very little literature addresses this question in comparison to addressing virtue in other helping professions. Several writers have attempted to specify the kind of virtues most consistent with the role and expectations of health care professionals, such as physicians and nurses, as well as psychotherapists and pastoral ministers. For instance, Tom Beauchamp and James Childress consider the virtues of compassion, discernment, trustworthiness, and

[26] James Keenan, *Goodness and Rightness in Thomas Aquinas's* Summa Theologiae (Washington, D.C.: Georgetown University Press, 1992).

[27] Elliot Cohen and Gale Cohen, *The Virtuous Therapist: Ethical Practice of Counseling and Psychotherapy* (Belmont, Calif.: Brooks/Cole, 1999); Richard Gula, *Ethics in Pastoral Ministry* (New York: Paulist Press, 1996).

[28] Gula, *Ethics in Pastoral Ministry,* 44.

integrity to be most compatible with the role and expectations of physicians, nurses, and other health care professionals.[29] Similarly, Naomi Meara, Lyle Schmidt, and Jeanne Day consider four similar virtues applicable to individuals practicing clinical and counseling psychology: prudence, integrity, respectfulness, and benevolence.[30] While Beauchamp and Childress[31] do not specify how their chosen set of virtues relate to the specific role expectations of health care providers, Meara, Schmidt, and Day[32] carefully delineate how their four virtues relate to the role expectations of counseling psychologists.

Gula offers a description of the virtuous pastoral minister.[33] He designates five virtues that are specifically related to the role expectations common to pastoral ministry personnel. Gula suggests that three of these virtues—holiness, love, and trustworthiness—are "covenantal" virtues, while the other two—altruism and prudence—are moral virtues.

A Taxonomy of Virtues

This book proposes that the following are requisite virtues for those undergoing pastoral counseling and spiritual direction as well as for those practicing pastoral counseling and spiritual direction: charity and holiness, prudence, self-care and compassion, trustworthiness, fidelity, justice, temperance, and physical fitness. The following descriptions of these requisite virtues are derived from the aforementioned works of Keenan and of Gula, as well as those of Bernard Haring.[34]

[29] Tom Beauchamp and James Childress, *Principles of Biomedical Ethics,* 4th ed. (New York: Oxford University Press, 1994).

[30] Naomi Meara, Lyle Schmidt, and Jeanne Day, "Principles and Virtues: A Foundation for Ethical Decisions, Policies, and Character," *The Counseling Psychologist* 24:1 (1996) 4–77.

[31] Beauchamp and Childress, *Principles of Biomedical Ethics.*

[32] Meara, Schmidt, and Day, "Principles and Virtues."

[33] Gula, *Ethics in Pastoral Ministry.*

[34] Bernard Haring, *The Virtues of an Authentic Life: A Celebration of Christian Maturity* (Liguori, Mo.: Liguori, 1997).

Charity and Holiness

Charity is the most basic of all virtues. Aquinas called it "the 'mother' of all virtues since all virtues are conceived within it."[35] Charity is more concerned with the interiority than with the outer world and external actions. It is the virtue that unites us to God, and is the very presence of God in our lives. While other virtues are acquired through practice, charity cannot be earned or learned since it is a freely given gift of God. Rather, we "grow in charity as we respond to it. Charity's daily urgings move us to be more considerate of an employee, to express more care for our family, and to face squarely our responsibilities."[36] Furthermore, charity enables us to curb our self-centeredness and reach out to others by prompting us to seek justice and fidelity in the world around us, while being vigilant against cowardice and intemperance.[37]

Very closely related to charity is the virtue of holiness. Holiness is the virtue that reflects the admonition "You shall be holy, for I am holy" (Lev 11:45). In ministry this means dedication to mediate the presence of God in one's environment and the commitment to work to establish right relationships with God, with others, and with creation. Holiness does not mean acting sanctimoniously or holding oneself out as superior to others. Rather, holiness recognizes our dependence on God as the source and center of life and wholeness.[38] Persons who manifest this virtue find strength, focus, and direction from a relationship of love with God as the center of their life. Holiness is living out of this center and staying in touch with this center through the practices of private prayer and public worship, as well as through the exercise of disciplines that express a life of ongoing conversion of thought and action.

Here are some indicators of the virtue of holiness in pastoral counselors and spiritual directors: (1) an openness to the

[35] Keenan, *Virtues for Ordinary Christians,* 49.

[36] Keenan, *Proposing Cardinal Virtues,* 50.

[37] Ibid.

[38] Gula, *Ethics in Pastoral Ministry.*

religious experience of others; (2) balance in life by cultivation of leisure and personal renewal through sabbaticals, retreats, and time off; (3) participation in communal prayer and private prayer; (4) an awareness of the presence of God in one's life; (5) development of talents in oneself and in others; (6) an attitude of detachment regarding material possessions.[39]

Prudence

Prudence is the virtue of discernment.[40] Unfortunately, prudence often is mistaken for cautious timidity and has the connotation of "being careful." Understood as the virtue of discernment, prudence is necessary to accurately assess, deliberate, and make decisions. Prudence listens to experience, it seeks counsel, and envisions the future to anticipate difficulties, to consider the consequences, and to be open to the unexpected. Then, it prayerfully considers these factors, resulting in a decision that is both true to the minister's self and fits the particular configuration of the situation under consideration.[41] Accordingly, prudence makes integrity possible by disallowing any split between the inner self and its outer expression in word and deed.

Manifestations of the virtue of prudence in pastoral counselors and spiritual directors include: (1) an openness to the experience of those whom one counsels or directs; (2) receptivity to the theoretical and professional developments in pastoral counseling and spiritual direction; (3) the daily practice of silence and stillness; (4) the discipline of self-reflection; and (5) decision-making accomplished in a strategic and timely fashion.[42]

Self-Care and Compassion

While the virtue of justice is about being concerned that others are cared for and treated equally, the virtue of self-care is

[39] Ibid.

[40] Ibid.

[41] Ibid.

[42] Ibid.

about taking care of oneself. Keenan originally called self-care the virtue of self-esteem.[43] However, he changed it to self-care as he recognized that self-care encompasses self-esteem as well as other factors that relate to taking responsibility for one's own psychological health and well-being. In other words, self-care is actually about self-love.[44] Balancing self-love is love and concern for the other, which is called compassion.

The virtue of compassion, or compassionate love, is the kind of love Jesus modeled through the service he gave to others in responding to his experience of God's love. It is the kind of love which meets the Johannine criterion: "By this everyone will know that you are my disciples, if you have love for one another" (John 13:35). Compassion is the virtue which enables ministers to value others as an end rather than as some utilitarian means to the minister's own end. Empathy, the capacity to enter, understand, and respond to another's frame of reference, is central to compassion. Shelton posits that empathy should be the heart of Christian ethics.[45]

The heart of the virtue of compassion is to live patiently with others while seeking their well-being. This requires that pastoral counselors and spiritual directors attend to their own physical, emotional, spiritual, and moral health. Staying healthy permits ministers to accept themselves so they can then be present to others without projecting their own needs, fears, and illusions. The virtuous love of self also includes love of neighbor. Appropriate love of self frees the minister to meet the needs of the vulnerable. Finally, compassion is the capacity to participate in the joys and sorrows of others without becoming overwhelmed by or lost in their experience.

Indicators of the virtues of self-care and compassion in pastoral counselors and spiritual directors include: (1) the practice of self-care in one's life and advocating it to those to

[43] Keenan, *Virtues for Ordinary Christians*.

[44] Ibid.

[45] Charles Shelton, *Morality of the Heart: A Psychology for the Christian Moral Life* (New York: Crossroads, 1990).

whom one ministers; (2) the recognition and acceptance of one's limitations, anger, fears, and hurts; (3) a reasonable degree of self-esteem; (4) the capacity for active listening and openness to those whom one counsels or directs; (5) the capacity to understand and reflect what another is experiencing without blame, judgment, or projection.[46]

Trustworthiness

The virtue of trustworthiness is a facet of the virtue of justice. Trustworthiness involves acting fairly and justly in a relationship with another. In a ministry setting, people expect ministers to be trustworthy. Gula notes that "trustworthiness is especially sought in ministers because they are looked upon as being entrusted by God."[47] Therefore, a breach of the sacred trust between a client or parishioner and a pastoral minister reflects a lack or loss of trustworthiness. Consequently, trustworthiness encompasses the practice of such virtues as honesty, fairness, truthfulness, loyalty, dependability, and humility. Gula adds that it is "unthinkable that one can be successful in ministry without being trustworthy."[48] He contends that being betrayed by a minister is often experienced as being betrayed by the church, or even by God.

Some indicators of trustworthiness in pastoral counselors and spiritual directors are: (1) respect for physical and emotional boundaries in minister–client/parishioner relationships; (2) respect for privacy and confidentiality; (3) recognition of the limits of one's own competence and appropriate referral-making when necessary; (4) maintenance of professional skills and knowledge through study, supervision, and consultation; (5) sustained commitments to professional activities and to personal relationships.[49]

[46] Gula, *Ethics in Pastoral Ministry.*

[47] Ibid., 47–8.

[48] Ibid., 47.

[49] Ibid.

Fidelity

While justice is the virtue of treating others equally, fidelity is the virtue of treating particular relationships preferentially. Fidelity is about treating those to whom one is closely related, i.e., friends, spouse, children, community members, etc., with special care and concern. Keenan proposes that fidelity is the first of the cardinal virtues that Christians are called to develop.[50]

Fidelity can be thought of as a type of friendship. A review of their teachings shows that Aristotle, Augustine, and Aquinas considered friendship the key to the moral life. Keenan indicates that in Jesus' life friendship was a central virtue, for not only did Jesus teach and heal others, he enjoyed spending time with people, particularly those who were special friends such as Mary, Martha, and Lazarus. Keenan also points out that fidelity to relationships requires considerable effort. It means practicing ways of communicating, sharing, being with, and giving and taking. More specifically, "we may need to make more calls, write more letters, take more strolls, linger a little longer with a friend. We may also need to disengage ourselves from the habit of counting or measuring what 'the other' does or does not."[51]

Clearly, pastoral counselors and spiritual directors need to make the practice of the virtue of fidelity a priority in their lives. To the extent that they do so, the matter of maintaining proper boundaries—as discussed with regard to the virtue of trustworthiness—should be less complicated and problematic. Ordinarily, this means that the counselor or director differentiates relationships such as those one maintains with a basic support system of family, peers, and close friends, and does not expect those to whom one ministers to function as one's basic support system.

Some indicators of the virtue of fidelity in pastoral counselors and spiritual directors are: (1) balances time and emotional

[50] Keenan, *Virtues for Ordinary Christians.*

[51] Ibid., 62.

energy between professional demands and the need to maintain and nurture significant relationships; particularly if the counselor or director is married and/or supporting family members, fidelity can require, on occasion, placing the family's needs above professional demands; (2) plans and takes time for family and close personal and intimate friends; (3) plans and takes time to be with and to emotionally support colleagues and professional peers; (4) is friendly, respectful, and caring to one's clients, maintaining appropriate boundaries and not expecting them to meet one's needs for emotional closeness.

Justice

Justice is the virtue of fairness which abhors special and preferential treatment. As such, it can sometimes be at odds with the virtue of fidelity. Justice is about treating others fairly, as well as recognizing unfairness in the world around us. The virtue of justice requires that an individual acquire a sense of fairness and become proficient in discerning the common good. It is not dependent on the law; as Keenan notes, simply because a nation does not outlaw an activity does not mean that the activity is fair and just.[52] For example, racism has been fostered by the legal systems of many Western nations. Even with the declaration of the Emancipation Proclamation and passage of the Voting Rights Act of 1965, legal remedies for racism have not been successful in eliminating racism in the United States today. Among other things, this situation suggests that the virtue of justice cannot be legislated.

Finally, acquiring the virtue of justice requires considerable practice. "We learn to determine justice and injustice by developing ourselves. The more we act for the common good by being inclusive and letting others speak for themselves, the more we can learn about the people whom we ought to become. Adults learn [about justice], as do children, through practice."[53]

[52] Ibid.

[53] Ibid., 69.

Practicing the virtue of justice in a pastoral counseling and spiritual direction setting is complicated in an America where poverty continues to coexist with accumulating wealth. Since pastoral counseling and spiritual direction have increasingly become fee-based professional services—rather than being provided gratis to parishioners—access to pastoral counseling and spiritual direction is increasingly limited to those who can afford professional fees. The challenge for pastoral counselors and spiritual directors, whose livelihood depends on a salary or professional fees, is to extend their services to a wide range of clients irrespective of their capacity to pay.

Some indicators of justice in pastoral counselors and spiritual directors are: (1) awareness of the systemic causes of injustice in the community in which the counselor or director practices; (2) advocacy of the principles of fairness in counseling or consultation sessions; (3) voting and encouraging others to vote in local and national elections; (4) and, most importantly, the establishment of a sliding fee arrangement and scheduling a given amount of pro bono sessions a month so that those with limited or no financial means have access to pastoral counseling or spiritual direction.

Fortitude and Courage

Fortitude is the virtue that "ensures firmness in difficulties and constancy in the pursuit of good."[54] This virtue enables one to face trials, persecutions, and even death. Fortitude strengthens one's resolve to resist temptation as well as to overcome obstacles in the moral domain of life. Furthermore, this virtue predisposes individuals to sacrifice their lives for a just cause.

Closely related to fortitude is the virtue of courage. Haring notes that courage is the virtue of boldness and "strength of soul," which is manifest by "strong-hearted and bold-spirited love."[55] Courage provides individuals the "strength to endure

[54] *Catechism of the Catholic Church* (Washington, D.C.: United States Catholic Conference, 1994) 444.

[55] Haring, *The Virtues of an Authentic Life,* 42–3.

stress and pressure with grace."[56] Furthermore, courage prompts individuals to right action in the face of personal or professional risks they might otherwise avoid. While courage requires confidence and braveness, it does not imply that the individual is fearless or reckless. Accordingly, Aristotle contends that courage is a disposition to feel appropriate degrees of both fear and confidence in challenging situations and to stand one's ground, to move forward, or retreat as the virtue of wisdom dictates.[57] Fortitude and courage are virtues that are not ordinarily associated with the practice of pastoral counseling or spiritual direction, given that pastoral counselors and spiritual directors are viewed as individuals who are empathic, nonjudgmental, and supportive. Nevertheless, both virtues have a place in the holistic, integrative practice of pastoral counseling or spiritual direction.

Some indicators of fortitude and courage for spiritual directors and pastoral counselors are: (1) the willingness to address moral issues over which the client or directee expresses reluctance but are necessary for growth; (2) the resolve to continue advocating for client rights in the face of negative professional consequences, e.g., a reprimand by clinic management or possible removal from a managed care provider panel; (3) the willingness to report a colleague to the appropriate professional organization for an ethics violation while one's colleagues appear to be unaffected.[58]

Temperance

Temperance is traditionally described as the virtue that balances one's concupiscent appetites, i.e., the desire to experience the good of food, drink, or sex. Thomas Aquinas clarifies

[56] James Drane, *Becoming a Good Doctor: The Place of Virtue and Character in Medical Ethics* (Kansas City, Mo.: Sheed & Ward, 1988) 158.

[57] Aristotle, *The Nicomachean Ethics,* trans. with an intro. by D. Ross (Oxford: Oxford University Press, 1951).

[58] Keenan, *Virtues for Ordinary Christians.*

that temperance "is not the repression of the desire for sensual pleasure but rather its tempering in the service of human growth."[59] Richard McBrien adds that from the patristic period temperance has been associated with Christian asceticism, which today is increasingly understood as not only moderation in behavior but also acceptance of one's self and associated limitations and vulnerabilities, rather than simply denial, renunciation, or self-abnegation.

Keenan agrees with this more positive view of temperance by noting that it

> is about enjoying life. It is about our being able to experience our temperaments as best as we can. . . . We are temperate people when we hit our stride. Temperance is living the life of constant exercises that keep our sensibilities, feelings, inclinations, hungers, and urges well toned and tuned.[60]

He also emphasizes the social dimension of intemperance by noting that secrecy and social isolation are associated with intemperances such as "secretive" alcohol and food binges.

Because ministry personnel have in the past tended to foster and promote body-denying ascetical practices spiritualities, the standard of love and the practice of honoring the body are important correctives for a more balanced understanding of the virtue of temperance. Haring adds an oft forgotten dimension to temperance as moderation which is the standard of love, i.e., love being the criterion for the goodness and rightness of actions. He is quite insistent on this point stating that, unless we bring the standard of love to all our desires and concupiscences, "we can never grow in the love of God and our neighbor."[61] Stephanie Paulsell highlights the importance of the Christian practice of honoring the body in light of moderation and the standard of love. In contrast to the body-denying practices associated with a negative view of asceticism and

[59] McBrien, *Catholicism,* 949.

[60] Keenan, *Virtues for Ordinary Christians,* 94–5.

[61] Haring, *The Virtues of an Authentic Life,* 45.

human flesh, the body is better understood as the temple of the Spirit and thus "worthy of care and blessing and ought never to be degraded or exploited. . . . The practice of honoring the body challenges us to remember the sacredness of the body in every moment of our lives."[62] She also notes that honoring the body is a shared practice, requiring the participation of the community in concern for all of creation. She insists that this practice "leads us to prophetic action by forming us as persons who love every human body and the ravaged body of the earth itself."[63]

Some indicators of temperance for spiritual directors and pastoral counselors are: (1) self-acceptance of one's body; (2) modeling appropriate ways of honoring the body to clients; (3) ascetical practices that are informed by the standard of love rather than avoidance of commitment or social isolation; (4) modeling an appropriate balance between intimacy and celibacy.

Physical Fitness

Keenan describes physical fitness as a virtue and believes it is a particularly important one for Christians. He notes that individuals are made in God's image and that a central Christian belief is the resurrection of the body. Nevertheless, he believes that today Christians are "too disembodied. We think virtue is not about the body, but about the soul, charity, faith, justice, sympathy. But our forbearers [*sic*] knew that the work of virtue penetrated the entire fabric of a human being: the whole heart, the whole mind, the whole body, the whole soul."[64] Regular exercise, adequate sleep, effective stress management, and appropriate nutrition are all part of physical fitness. Adequate physical fitness is related to a sense of physical well-being.

[62] Stephanie Paulsell, "Honoring the Body," *Practicing Our Faith: A Way of Life for a Searching People,* ed. Dorothy Bass (San Francisco: Jossey-Bass, 1997) 15.

[63] Ibid, 16.

[64] Keenan, *Virtues for Ordinary Christians,* 135.

Generally speaking, pastoral counselors and spiritual directors tend not to be paragons of physical well-being. To the extent that counselors and directors make no effort to become more physically fit and role model this virtue for their clients, they are probably lacking in the virtue of physical fitness.

Some indicators of the virtue of physical fitness in pastoral counselors and spiritual directors are: (1) maintaining a healthy diet and a reasonable weight; (2) ensuring a balanced daily schedule of adequate sleep, relaxation, exercise fitness, and stress management activities; and (3) role-modeling physical health and well-being and advocating a healthy embodied spirituality to their clients.

The Virtue Ethics Perspective in Spiritual Direction and Pastoral Counseling

Presumably professional spiritual directors and pastoral counselors are enjoined by the codes of ethics of their professional organizations to act ethically in their professional roles. Professional codes of ethics are not intended to address all possible ethical matters. Since increasing numbers of clients expect that helping professionals will assist them with moral issues and dilemmas, it would not be unreasonable to anticipate that spiritual seekers and other clients with religious issues may need to or want to address either ethical or moral matters in the course of therapy. Many questions arise. Is it ethical for directors and counselors to discuss such matters? Should spiritual seekers and other clients be counseled to act ethically in their professional and personal lives? Is it or might it be unethical for a spiritual director or pastoral counselor to broach some ethical matters with spiritual seekers? Obviously, there are no easy answers to these questions. An ethical perspective is much broader than the provisions of a code of ethics.

Developing an ethical perspective involves not only learning ethical theories and principles but also incorporating such principles in one's own philosophy of life and then acting on these principles in one's daily personal and professional life. It means becoming a person of good character, i.e., someone who acts virtuously. In other words, developing an ethical perspective means becoming a "virtuous" spiritual director or pastoral counselor.

The ethical theory that emphasizes character and virtue is virtue ethics. Virtue ethics defines certain traits of character which are understood to make one a morally good person. Hauerwas states that Christian ethics "is best understood as an ethics of character since the Christian moral life is fundamentally an orientation of the person."[65] He insists that the focus of morality must shift from an individual's external behavior and rules to the person's internal dispositions and character.

While rule and principle ethics focus on morally good actions, virtue ethics focuses on morally good character. For virtue ethics the question is not: Is this action moral? Rather, it is: What kind of person am I becoming by doing this or that action? According to virtue ethics, moral virtues are states of character concerned with controlling and directing not only one's thoughts and rational processes but also one's emotions and feeling. The repeated performance of virtuous actions leads to the acquisition of virtue. The morally virtuous person aims at morally good ends rather at being clever and goal-oriented.

How do we define a virtuous spiritual director and a virtuous pastoral counselor? Virtuous therapists are professional individuals of good moral character whose actions reflect both the practice of virtue and the ability to incorporate professional standards in daily practice. They not only practice virtue but model it in their personal and professional lives. "A morally virtuous psychotherapist would seek to be honest with her clients not merely because this behavior is itself a way toward the goal of maximizing profit—supposing that 'morality pays' by attracting clients—but because honesty itself is to be valued."[66] These authors contend that a rule or principle ethics,

[65] Hauerwas, *Character and the Christian Life*, vii.

[66] Cohen and Cohen, *The Virtuous Therapist*, 19–20.

i.e., the framework for professional codes of ethics, is a woefully inadequate basis for the ethical practice of counseling and psychotherapy. Instead, they propose a composite ethical theory that recognizes that moral action involves not only rules or professional standards but also emotions, human relatedness, virtue, and sensitivity to the nuances of a specific individual context.

In short, virtuous spiritual directors and pastoral counselors practice and model virtue in their personal and professional lives as well as incorporate professional ethical standards in their clinical work.

Concluding Note

After a brief description of the moral domain of life, this chapter went on to focus on character and virtue. Their relationship and the recent retrieval of the character/virtue tradition in moral theology and in psychology were detailed. Regarding the moral domain and practice, an important distinction was made between merely complying with an ethics code and becoming virtuous spiritual directors and pastoral counselors. In addition, various efforts to classify virtues culminated in a taxonomy of virtues applicable to the practice of spiritual direction and pastoral counseling. This taxonomy of virtues is a key component in the holistic and integrative model proposed in Chapter 6.

5

Psychological Perspectives on Transformation

The psychological domain is integrally related to the spiritual and moral domains as well as the meta-domain of transformation. The perspective one has about the psychological domain and the dimensions of transformation influence one's view of spiritual direction and pastoral counseling. The criticism that most pastoral counseling and spiritual direction is reductionistic has been directed largely to overemphasis on the psychological domain and the over-reliance on psychological constructs.

This chapter briefly describes the psychological domain of life and then shifts to the complex relationship between psychology and spirituality and psychology and the moral constructs of character and virtue. Self-theory, which is most useful in understanding the journey from the false self to the true self, is described in some detail. Finally, a taxonomy of self-capacities is presented.

The Psychological Domain of Life

The psychological domain includes all affective or emotional functioning and well-being, as well as all aspects of cognitive abilities and functioning. Western culture has been significantly impacted by the psychological imagination, that is, by the pervasive way in which Westerners perceive, think, and act upon reality with psychological categories and explanations. Today, it is difficult to imagine discussing spirituality in the absence of psychological categories.

Relationship Between Psychology and Spirituality

Today, there is an emerging consensus, particularly among advocates of transpersonal psychology, that "the psychological and spiritual dimensions of human experience are different, though at times overlapping, with the spiritual as foundational."[1] In its earliest formulation, transpersonal psychology assumed that the psychological and spiritual lines of development were identical or formed one continuous line or spectrum.[2] It was also assumed that an individual would first pursue psychological integration and then move on to spiritual integration. Usually that meant beginning in psychotherapy and, when that was successfully completed, taking up spiritual practices and working with a spiritual guide. Basically, it was believed that only those who were sufficiently healed and psychologically integrated were capable of true spiritual development and realization.

Such beliefs do not match current clinical research and clinical practice. Some clients with highly advanced spiritual development may function at primitive levels psychologically and interpersonally, while psychological development far exceeds spiritual development in others. Then there are other clients where spiritual and psychological development is more balanced. Similarly, history records a number of disturbed, psychotic, and neurotic saints and spiritually advanced individuals. Furthermore, to presume that all saints, sages, and shamans throughout history have somehow spontaneously

[1] Brant Cortright, *Psychotherapy and Spirit: Theory and Practice in Transpersonal Psychotherapy* (Albany: State University of New York Press, 1997) 237.

[2] Ken Wilber, *The Spectrum of Consciousness* (Wheaton, Ill.: Quest, 1977).

achieved a working through of childhood traumas and unconscious defenses leading to a high level of psychological integration prior to their spiritual development is extremely dubious.[3]

Transpersonally-oriented clinicians have observed that psychological and spiritual developments are composed of multiple and complex developmental pathways that mutually interact but are different. In other words, the spiritual emerges in and through psychological work rather than after it. Furthermore, clinicians espousing a transpersonal approach to psychotherapy tend to view their work within a context of spiritual unfolding, since the basic assumption of transpersonal psychology is that individuals are spiritual beings rather than simply a psychological ego. Another basic tenet of transpersonal psychology is that achieving psychological integration is not essential for spiritual realization, nor does spiritual realization bring about psychological integration. Nevertheless, psychotherapy can be quite helpful for those on the spiritual journey in contending with avoidances and unconscious defenses, just as the inner growth resulting from spiritual practices can be helpful in one's psychological work. In short, each can help the other but neither one is required for advance in the other.[4]

Clinicians practicing transpersonal psychotherapy note that it is possible to pursue psychological wholeness and spiritual wholeness simultaneously, and that while "one or the other may predominate at times, it is a both/and process rather than an either/or or even first one/then the other."[5] Psychotherapy may facilitate spiritual unfolding more skillfully than spiritual practices alone since psychotherapy can effectively break through unconscious and defensive patterns which may be imprisoning spirit energy. Finally, since it aims at expanding consciousness, psychotherapy can be thought of as a spiritual activity of sorts.

[3] Cortright, *Psychotherapy and Spirit.*

[4] Ibid.

[5] Ibid., 234.

Psychological Perspective on Character

Character has a long and venerable tradition in the study of personality "which can be traced to the early Greeks."[6] Although there was a biological tradition in the study of personality that emphasized temperament, the psychological tradition that emphasized character was in vogue for the first two-thirds of the twentieth century. Currently, personality is being conceptualized in a broader perspective and has come to be described as the confluence of both character and temperament.[7]

There is an extraordinary line of psychological research on character that appears to validate the description of moral character as described above by Donald Gelpi[8] and implied by Stanley Hauerwas[9] and William Brown.[10] C. Robert Cloninger and his colleagues have found that individuals with mature personalities or character structures tend to be self-responsible, cooperative, and self-transcendent.[11] Gelpi's description involved both self-responsibility and the capacity for life-giving relationship, which is related to cooperation.[12] Furthermore, Gelpi's description of conversion implies self-transcendence. In contrast, Cloninger et al. note that those with personality or character disorders are noted to have difficulty with self-acceptance, were intolerant and revengeful toward others, and felt self-conscious

[6] Theodore Millon, *Disorders of Personality: DSM-IV and Beyond,* 2d ed. (New York: Wiley, 1996) 35.

[7] Len Sperry, "Leadership Dynamics: Character and Character Structure in Executives," *Consulting Psychology Journal* 49 (1997) 268.

[8] Donald Gelpi, *The Conversion Experience: A Reflective Guide for RCIA Participants and Others* (New York: Paulist Press, 1998).

[9] Stanley Hauerwas, *Character and the Christian Life: A Study in Theological Ethics* (Notre Dame, Ind.: University of Notre Dame Press, 1975).

[10] William Brown, *Character in Crisis: A Fresh Approach to the Wisdom Literature of the Old Testament* (Grand Rapids, Mich.: Eerdmans, 1996).

[11] C. Robert Cloninger, Dragan Svrakic, and Thomas Pryzbeck, "A Psychobiological Model of Temperament and Character," *Archives of General Psychiatry* 50 (1993) 975–90.

[12] Gelpi, *The Conversion Experience,* 1998.

and unfulfilled.[13] This suggested that the presence or absence of a personality disorder could be defined in terms of the character dimensions of self-directedness or responsibility, cooperativeness, and self-transcendence.[14]

Self-Directedness

The basic concept of self-directedness refers to self-determination, which is an individual's ability to control, regulate, and adapt behavior in accord with one's chosen goals and values. Individuals differ in their capacity for self-determination. Individuals with moderate to high levels of self-determination are considered to be mature, effective, and well-organized people who exhibit self-esteem, are able to admit faults and accept themselves as they are, feel their lives have meaning and purpose, can delay gratification in order to achieve their goals, and take initiative in overcoming challenges. On the other hand, individuals with lower levels of self-determination have low self-esteem, blame others for their problems, feel uncertain of their identity or purpose, and are often reactive, dependent, and without resources.

Self-determination can be thought of as having various sub-components such as internal locus of control, purposefulness, resourcefulness, and self-efficacy. Individuals with an internal locus of control tend to believe that their success is controlled by their own efforts, whereas individuals with an external locus of control tend to believe their success is controlled by factors outside themselves. Research on locus of control indicates that those with an internal locus of control are more responsible and resourceful problem-solvers, whereas others are more alienated and apathetic, tending to blame other people and chance circumstances for problems.

Purposefulness and meaningful goal-direction is a motivating force in mature people. Such purposefulness varies

[13] Cloninger, Svrakic, and Pryzbeck, "A Psychobiological Model."
[14] Ibid., 975.

widely between individuals. Initiative and resourceful problem-solving, which define effective executives, are important aspects of mature character. Self-efficacy is also related to resourcefulness and initiative in goal-directed behavior.

Self-esteem and the ability to accept one's limitations unapologetically without fantasies of unlimited ability and ageless youth are crucial aspects of the development of mature self-directed behavior. Individuals with poor adjustment and feelings of inferiority or inadequacy are often reactive and deny, repress, or ignore their faults, wishing to be best at everything always, whereas well adjusted individuals are able to recognize and admit unflattering truths about themselves. Such positive self-esteem and ability to accept individual limitations is strongly correlated with responsibility and resourcefulness. The absence of self-directedness is the common characteristic of all categories of personality disorder. Regardless of other personality traits or circumstances, a personality disorder is likely to be present if self-directedness is low.

Considered as a developmental process, self-directedness has various dimensions or indicators. These indicators can be understood as reflecting a continuum of health or high functioning health to disorder or low functioning, and conceivably a virtue/vice continuum. Five dimensions or indicators were proposed by Cloninger: responsible vs. blaming; purposeful vs. goal-less; resourceful vs. passive; self-accepting vs. wishful; and disciplined vs. undisciplined.[15]

Cooperativeness

The character factor of cooperativeness was formulated to account for individual differences in identification with and acceptance of other people. This factor is a measure of character that is related to agreeability vs. self-centered aggression and hostility. Low cooperativeness scores contribute substantially to the likelihood of a concomitant personality disorder.

[15] Cloninger, Svrakic, and Pryzbeck, "A Psychobiological Model."

In individuals who are high or only moderately low in self-directedness, the probability of a diagnosis of personality disorder was increased by low cooperativeness. All categories of personality disorder are associated with low cooperativeness. Cooperative individuals tend to be socially tolerant, empathic, helpful, and compassionate, while uncooperative individuals tend to be socially intolerant, disinterested in other people, unhelpful, and revengeful. Cooperative individuals are likely to show unconditional acceptance of others, empathy with other's feelings, and willingness to help others achieve their goals without selfish domination. It is not surprising that social acceptance, helpfulness, and concern for the rights of others are correlated with positive self-esteem. Empathy, which is a feeling of unity or identification with others, facilitates improved communication and compassion. Helpful generativity and compassion are frequently noted as signs of maturity in developmental psychology. For instance, such compassion involves the willingness to forgive and be kind to others regardless of their behavior, rather than to seek revenge or to enjoy their embarrassment or suffering; it involves feelings of brotherly love and the absence of hostility. Mature persons are more likely to seek mutually satisfying "win-win" solutions to problems than indulge personal gain. Finally, religious traditions also emphasize the notion of "pure-hearted" acceptance of principles that cannot be broken without the inevitability of grave consequences for individuals and society.

Considered as a developmental process, self-transcendence has various dimensions or indicators. These indicators can be understood as reflecting a continuum from health or high functioning health to disorder or low functioning, and conceivably a virtue/vice continuum. Five dimensions or indicators were proposed by Cloninger: tender-hearted vs. intolerant; empathic vs. insensitive; helpful vs. selfish; compassionate vs. revengeful; and principled vs. opportunistic.[16]

[16] Ibid.

Self-Transcendence

Self-transcendence and character traits associated with spirituality are typically neglected in systematic research and omitted from personality inventories. Nevertheless, observations about self-transcendence and self-actualization abound. Specifically, the subjective experiences and changes in behavior of people who attain the state of self-transcendence as a result of insight and meditation techniques have been well documented in the transpersonal psychology literature. The stable self-forgetfulness of self-transcendent individuals has been described as the same as experienced transiently when individuals are totally absorbed, intensely concentrated, and fascinated by one thing, such that they may forget where they are and lose all sense of the passage of time. Such absorption often leads to "transpersonal" identification with things outside of the individual self. The person may identify or feel a sense of spiritual union with anything or everything. The stable self-forgetfulness of self-transcendent people has been described as the same as experienced transiently by people when they are totally absorbed, intensely concentrated, and fascinated by one thing. In such one-pointed concentration, people may forget where they are and lose all sense of the passage of time.

Self-transcendence is considerably lower in psychiatric in-patients than in adults in the general community. Except for individuals with schizoid and schizotypal personality disorder, self-transcendence was not a distinguishing factor between patients with and without personality disorders. Self-transcendence can be particularly useful in distinguishing schizoid from schizotypal patients because the latter tend to endorse questions about extrasensory perception and other aspects of self-transcendence. Also, individuals with schizoid personality disorder tended to exhibit with low self-transcendence. In contrast, self-directedness and cooperativeness were low in all personality disorders.[17] Thus, it appears that psycho-

[17] D. Svrakic, C. Whitehead, T. Pryzbeck, and R. Cloninger, "Differential Diagnosis of Personality Disorders by the Seven-Factor Model of

logically healthy spiritual seekers manifest considerably more self-transcendence than less mature individuals.

Considered as a developmental process, self-transcendence has various dimensions or indicators. These indicators can be understood as reflecting a continuum from health or high functioning to disorder or low functioning, and conceivably a virtue—vice continuum. Five dimensions or indicators were proposed by Cloninger: imaginative vs. conventional; intuitive vs. logical; acquiescent vs. doubtful; spiritual vs. materialistic; and idealistic vs. relativistic.[18]

The Scientific Study of Virtue

As noted earlier, a post-modern critique of contemporary psychology and psychotherapy makes a compelling case that there can never be a value-free psychology or psychotherapy and that psychology would do well to reconsider its relationship with moral philosophy. In a somewhat related vein, major figures in the psychology research community are beginning to retrieve psychology's early interest in character and virtue.[19] This retrieval effort is being called "positive psychology." Positive psychology refers to an emphasis on strengths and the developmental or growth model rather than on the dark side of psychology with its emphasis on human foibles and the disease or psychopathology model. In other words, much of contemporary psychology and psychotherapy has become preoccupied with healing and "concentrates on repairing damage within a disease model of human functioning. This almost exclusive attention to pathology neglects the fulfilled individual and the thriving community."[20] One wonders how it is that the social

---

Temperament and Character," *Archives of General Psychiatry* 50 (1993) 991–9.

[18] Cloninger, Svrakic, and Pryzbeck, "A Psychobiological Model."

[19] Michael McCullough and C. R. Snyder, "Classical Sources of Human Strength: Revisiting an Old House and Building a New One," *Journal of Social and Clinical Psychology* 19 (2000) 2.

[20] Martin Seligman and Mihaly Czsikszentmihaly, "Positive Psychology: An Introduction," *American Psychologist* 55 (2000) 5.

sciences, particularly psychology, have come to "view the human strengths and virtues—altruism, courage, honesty, duty, joy, health, responsibility and good cheer—as derivative, defensive or downright illusions, while weakness and negative motivations—anxiety, lust, selfishness, paranoia, anger, disorder and sadness—are viewed as authentic?"[21] The aim of the field of positive psychology "is to begin to catalyze a change in the focus of psychology not only with repairing the worst things in life to also building positive qualities."[22]

Three pillars have been proposed for positive psychology: subjective well-being, positive character, and positive community. Subjective well-being includes contentment, satisfaction, hope, and optimism; positive character includes "the capacity for love and vocation, courage, interpersonal skill, aesthetic sensibility, perseverance, forgiveness, originality, future mindedness, spirituality, high talent and wisdom."[23] Finally, positive community includes "the civic virtues and the institutions that move individuals toward better citizenship: responsibility, nurturance, altruism, civility, moderation, tolerance and work ethic."[24]

From a psychological perspective, virtues are defined "as any psychological process that enables a person to think and act so as to benefit both him- or herself and society."[25] This is similar to Roberts' proposition that "virtues operate to help a person to live well among people."[26] This dual emphasis on individual and community is notably distinct from the implicit or explicit advocacy of radical individualism characteristic of much of contemporary psychology and psychotherapy. Like

[21] Martin Seligman, "Positive Social Science," *Journal of Positive Behavior Interventions* 1 (1999) 181.

[22] Seligman and Czsikszentmihaly, "Positive Psychology," 5.

[23] Ibid.

[24] Ibid.

[25] McCullough and Snyder, "Classical Sources of Human Strength," 1.

[26] Quoted by C. R. Snyder and M. McCullough, "A Positive Psychology of Dreams: 'If You Build It, They Will Come . . . ,'" *Journal of Social and Clinical Psychology* 19:1 (2000) 151–60.

Aristotle, those advocating positive psychology emphasize thriving or flourishing as the result of virtuous living.

While some humanistic psychologies have also championed human strengths and self-actualization over the past four decades, only positive psychology has endeavored to achieve a scientific understanding and effective interventions to achieve virtue and human flourishing. A special issue of the *Journal of Social and Clinical Psychology* edited by Michael McCullough and C. R. Snyder consists of articles describing the current state of research data and findings on seven virtues: self-control, hope, forgiveness, gratitude, humility, wisdom, and love.[27]

Virtue as a Dimension of Personality

Roy Baumeister and Julie Exline have offered a psychological framework for understanding virtue as a key dimension of personality.[28] Their basic assumption is the social nature of human existence wherein individuals are motivated by the basic need to belong and the universality of group life. Personality is understood as adaptation to the requirements of living among others. If the need to belong were the only human motivation, then morality and virtue might not be difficult to achieve. Unfortunately, however, the potential for conflict between individuals is inherent in group life.

Baumeister and Exline define "morality as a set of rules that enable individuals to live together in harmony and virtue is an internalization of moral rules."[29] Hence virtuous people should make the best citizens and relationship partners, because they will not let their own wishes cause actions that are detrimental to other people or to the group or community.

[27] Michael McCullough and C. R. Snyder, eds., special issue on Virtues, *Journal of Social and Clinical Psychology* 19 (2000).

[28] Roy Baumeister and Julie Exline, "Virtue, Personality and Social Relations: Self-Control the Moral Muscle," *Journal of Personality* 67:6 (1999) 1165–94.

[29] Ibid., 1166.

They point to research on the interpersonal nature of guilt to support the view that moral traits must be understood in the context of social relations. Likewise, if morality depends on social relations, then changes in the nature of social relations can necessitate the development of other virtues to sustain the relationship. Baumeister and Exline describe three aspects of modern Western social life that have created a social environment that is especially inhospitable to virtue. First, the rising instability of social relationships has weakened the social forces that penalize immoral behavior. Second, new economic patterns depend on the pursuit of self-interest to achieve benefits to the collective. Third, the rising moral ideology of selfhood has re-categorized many aspects of what constitutes self-interest and goodness, a change that undermines the age-old opposition between self and morality.

Baumeister and Exline contend that the central challenge for developing a personality theory of virtue is to understand how individuals manage to override their own selfish inclinations and do what is socially desirable and expected. They propose that the most relevant work in psychology is the study of self-control and self-regulation. Self-regulation is the process by which the self alters its own responses.

According to them self-control appears to be the core dynamic of both vices and virtues. Vice signifies failure of self-control, whereas virtue involves the consistent, disciplined exercise of self-control. Thus, they conclude that self-control can fairly be regarded as the master virtue.[30]

As for how self-control operates, recent research suggests that it is similar to a muscle, resembling the traditional concept of willpower. Individuals may vary in the strength of this moral muscle, and such individual differences will contribute to differences in virtue. Baumeister and Exline believe that a personality-based theory of virtue should recognize that the moral muscle is used for other acts of volition, such as responsible choice and active initiative, alongside self-control. Interestingly, they conclude that virtuous behavior may even "deterio-

[30] Ibid., 1170.

rate when people expend their strength in responsible decision-making. Exercising power and responsibility, making important decisions, dealing with stress and similar demands may deplete the resource and lead to moral deterioration."[31]

There appear to be other factors that contribute to differences in virtuous behavior. For example, morality depends on using one's self-regulatory strength in the service of conforming to moral standards. Thus, people who do not endorse moral standards may behave in immoral ways regardless of their degree of willpower. Likewise, monitoring is necessary for successful self-regulation. When people cease monitoring themselves, i.e., while intoxicated or "stoned," virtue may fail.

Psychology's quest to achieve value-neutrality in its pursuit of the scientific ideal has been a barrier to the study of virtue. Baumeister and Exline's theory of virtue has effectively surmounted this barrier. By positing self-control as the master virtue, personality research can study both processes and differences in moral traits in ways that are amenable to currently available research methods. Accordingly, virtue involves overcoming one's own undesirable dispositions in order to act in ways that will benefit others. The processes by which individuals alter their own behavior so as to behave in socially desirable ways can then be studied objectively. Conceivably such empirical research can positively impact the practice of spiritual direction and pastoral counseling.

Self-Theory

There is much in the Eastern and Western spiritual traditions and in psychological literature on the self. This section provides a brief overview of self-theory, then discusses and critiques self-transcendence, and finally describes self-capacities. James Masterson described an object-relations perspective on the self in his book *The Real Self*.[32] Essentially, the concept of

[31] Ibid., 1189.

[32] James Masterson, *The Real Self: A Developmental Self and Object Relations Approach* (New York: Brunner/Mazel, 1985).

the self can be understood in terms of related constructs such as self-image, self-representation, and self-organization, and contrasted with other constructs such as ego and identity. According to Masterson, self-image consists of the image that individuals have of themselves at a particular time and circumstance. Self-image consists of their body image as well as their mental representation at that time. This image may be conscious or unconscious, realistic or distorted. A self-representation, on the other hand, is constructed by the ego out of the many realistic and distorted self-images individuals have had at different times. It represents individuals as they consciously and unconsciously perceive themselves, and can be dormant or active. Masterson observes that subjective experience may be organized by multiple self-representations, that is, the "I" of one experience is not necessarily the same as the "I" of another experience. He uses the term "supraordinate self-organization" to refer to the organization, patterning, and connection of the various subordinate self-images and self-representations. Supraordinate self-organization provides a sense of continuity, unity, and wholeness among these images and representations.

The self and the ego typically develop and function in tandem wherein the self is the representational component of the ego and the ego is the executive component of the self. A developmental arrest of the ego means that the self will also be developmentally arrested. Masterson contends that ego identity is the ego's synthesizing power in the light of its central psychosocial function, while self-identity is the integration of the individual's self role images. Accordingly, one speaks of self-identity rather than ego-identity when referring to the I perceiving itself as uniform and continuous in time. The self is predominantly preconscious and conscious while the ego is predominantly unconscious.

Masterson contends that the process of self-development culminates in the identity crisis of adolescence, when the adolescent tests, selects, and integrates the self-images of childhood with the demands of adolescence and adulthood. Masterson notes that "the final self is fixed at the end of adolescence as superordinate to any single identification from the individual's childhood. Although it's fixed in terms of identification with childhood self-images, it still remains open to further development change."[33]

In short, he would contend that the development of the real self is largely completed by late adolescence or early adulthood. This contrasts with other theories of self-development, i.e., that of Carl Jung, Erik Erikson, Robert Kegan, Daniel Helminak, etc., that view self-development as extending into middle and late adulthood.

Furthermore, the self can also be differentiated into "true self" and "false self." From a clinical psychiatric or purely psychological perspective, the real self consists of the sum total of the intrapsychic images of the self and its associated object representations. The real self has two functions: it provides an emotional vehicle for self-expression and it operates to maintain self-esteem through the mastery of reality tasks. It is distinguished from the false self which is based on fantasy and which maintains self-esteem by defending against painful affects.[34]

From a psychospiritual perspective, Keating describes the false self as the self that develops to cope with the emotional trauma of early childhood.[35] It seeks happiness in satisfying the instinctual needs of survival, esteem, and control, and bases its self-worth on cultural or group identification. In contrast, the true self is one's participation in the divine life manifested in one's uniqueness. Thomas Merton's notion of the false self suggests that it is a failure in self-transcendence.[36] For most spiritual writers, the movement from the false self to the real or true self involves the process of self-transcendence.

[33] James Masterson, *The Personality Disorders* (Phoenix: Zieg/Tucker, 2000) 63.

[34] Ibid.

[35] Thomas Keating, *Invitation to Love: The Way of Christian Contemplation* (New York: Continuum, 1998).

[36] Thomas Merton, *New Seeds of Contemplation,* rev. ed. (New York: Norton, 1974).

Self-Transcendence Theory

Self-transcendence theory, particularly the theory articulated by Walter Conn,[37] has been described and critiqued in Chapter 2. Essentially, this book elaborates and revises Conn's formulation of self-transcendence as the psychological and spiritual theology foundation for spiritual direction and pastoral counseling. Conn posits self-transcendence as the most basic human desire and drive to move beyond or transcend the self. While having both a spiritual theology and psychological basis, Conn's self-transcendence theory is heavily dependent on theoretical constructs from both object-relations and self-psychology. Not surprisingly, this theory emphasizes an intrapsychic and interpersonal perspective and does not formally articulate the social, community, or character dimensions.

Furthermore, while Conn mentions "internal transformation" and "structural transformation," he does not define them but implies they are synonymous with self-transcendence.[38] While self-transcendence could be a synonym for self-transformation, self-transcendence cannot be synonymous with social transformation. I would contend that transformation is a broader construct than Conn's formulation of self-transcendence in that it includes both self transformation and social transformation.

In short, Conn's foundational formulation is the most sophisticated integration of psychological and theological constructs to date, yet it reflects many of the shortcomings of current practice. These shortcomings include an over-reliance on psychological constructs and an emphasis on the individual at the expense of the community and the socio-political dimension.

Even though pastoral counselors and spiritual directors may endorse this theory of self-transcendence for their practice, believing it is holistic and inclusive of all dimensions of

[37] Walter Conn, *The Desiring Self: Rooting Pastoral Counseling and Spiritual Direction in Self-Transcendence* (New York: Paulist Press, 1988).

[38] Ibid., 117–8.

human experience, their practice may actually be reductionistic in that some dimensions, most notably the moral and the sociopolitical dimensions, are minimized or ignored. However, this book contends that the goal of spiritual direction and pastoral counseling is both self and social transformation, and that all dimensions of transformation must be addressed.

A Taxonomy of Self-Capacities

The psychological domain, especially when viewed from a spiritual perspective, has traditionally emphasized self-theory. This emphasis, or over-emphasis, on self-theory has been the source of considerable criticism and concern. Nevertheless, the construct of self is intimately related to the construct of character, and both can be conceptualized as representing two sides of a coin. The most tangible aspect of self is self-capacity. Self-capacities are defined as requisite abilities that are essential for adequate personal functioning and adequate functioning in relationships and in the community.[39]

Individuals with a healthy real self are able to manage both the routine set backs in life as well as serious crises. The experience of personal, social, professional, or financial crises can be the occasion of growth for the healthy self, in contrast to the paralysis and defeat experienced by those with an impaired or false self. As the healthy self develops and becomes whole and autonomous, it can be characterized by a number of self-capacities. Masterson, in both *The Personality Disorders* and *The Real Self,* briefly describes ten such capacities derived from his clinical research. These were supplemented with three additional self-capacities in order to establish a taxonomy that correlated with the dimensions of transformation and the taxonomies of virtues and spiritual practices.

[39] Masterson, *The Real Self.*

Self-Mastery

This is the capacity in which the self has a sense of entitlement to appropriate experiences of pleasure and mastery in life. This capacity develops from early life experiences of mastery combined with the acknowledgment and support of the real self by parents and caretakers. This is not a self-contained capacity in that external input (i.e., rules, policies, medical advice, etc.) and support are necessary to balance inner desires and cravings. This sense of mastery and self-control extends to needs, desires, wishes, and cravings. This capacity is deficient in borderline personalities and over-inflated in narcissistic personalities.

Spontaneity

This is the capacity to experience a wide range of feelings appropriately, deeply, and without blocking or deadening the impact of the emotion. Specifically, it refers to a full, spontaneous expression of the feeling—whether it be anger, disappointment, or joy—that is appropriate and consistent with the situation or circumstance. Unlike the false self, the healthy real self accepts the wide range of feelings and is not afraid to express them. Even when accounting for the impact of character and temperament, there is an appropriate range of affects when the healthy self experiences a failed expectation, loss, or conflict.

Self-Activation

The capacity for self-activation is the ability to identify one's unique individuality, goals, dreams, and wishes, and then to be assertive in expressing them and achieving them. The evolving capacity for self-activation is essential in constellating one's identity and becoming one's own person.

Self-Acknowledgment

This capacity permits individuals to identify and acknowledge that they effectively coped with a crisis or concern in a positive, creative fashion. Rather than depending on others to refuel one's sense of self-esteem, it is the capacity to renew belief in one's own worthiness. Accordingly, individuals with this capacity have little need to act in an overly dependent or solicitous fashion in order to be liked, accepted, or considered worthy by others.

Self-Soothing

Self-soothing is the capacity to limit, minimize, and soothe painful affects. The healthy real self does not allow an individual to wallow in misery or abuse. It limits exposure to toxic and non-supportive relationships and circumstances, and soothes painful feelings when they arise without recourse to emotional numbing, feelings of inner emptiness, or depersonalization and derealization.

Self-Continuity

This is the capacity of the self to recognize and to acknowledge that the inner core of self persists and is continuous through space and over time. Despite one's moods, acceptance of success or failure, individuals with a healthy real self have an inner core, an "I," that remains the same even as they develop and grow.

Commitment

Commitment is the capacity for entrusting the self to a personal, community, or career goal or to a relationship and then to persevere in attaining it. Despite setbacks or obstacles, individuals with a healthy real self do not abandon a decision or a goal when it is good for them or for the community.

Creativity

This is the capacity to use the self to replace old familiar patterns with new, unique, and different patterns. It is also the capacity to rearrange characterological patterns that threaten to block self-expression, eliminate and replace false impressions with more accurate ones, and learn how to view threats and negative situations as opportunities for growth.

Intimacy

Intimacy is the capacity for expressing the self fully in a close relationship with minimal anxiety or fears about rejection. This requires the temporary suspension of personal boundaries while risking the sharing of one's deepest sense of self with trustworthy individuals. Individuals without a healthy real self, such as borderline personalities, can quickly engage in intimate behaviors and indiscriminately permit their interpersonal boundaries to be violated by others who may not be worthy of such trust.

Autonomy

The capacity for autonomy is the capacity to regulate affect and self-esteem freely with minimal fear of abandonment or engulfment. It is the ability to be alone while managing one's feelings and thoughts. It differs from psychic loneliness, which originates from the impaired real self and results in compulsive efforts to fill the pathological void with indiscriminate and destructive relationships or compulsive behaviors such as eating, substance use, or sexual activity. Autonomy, as noted earlier, is a key component of Conn's theory of self-transcendence.

Other Self-Capacities

The healthy, real self is characterized by the presence of these self-capacities in contrast to individuals with self-disorders, i.e., personality disorders, where many or most of these capacities are notably absent. While these ten self-capacities are necessary for psychological well-being, they are not sufficient for spiritual transformation or well-being. Three other self-capacities appear to be related to transformation. They are critical self-reflection, critical social consciousness, and self-surrender. Each is briefly defined.

Critical Reflection

Critical reflection is the capacity to objectively and systematically analyze ideas, ideologies, and situations and related underlying assumptions. It requires and builds on the requisite cognitive capacity to think abstractly, compare and contrast and develop alternative explanations. Critical reflection is a skill that is developed and honed by practice and applicability to progressively more complex situations or problems.

Critical Social Consciousness

Critical social consciousness is the capacity to analyze social and organizational situations and dynamics in terms of ethical and moral assumptions and consequences. It requires and builds on the capacity for critical reflection. Like critical reflection, critical social consciousness is a skill that is developed and honed by practice and applicability to progressively more complex situations.

Self-Surrender

Self-surrender is the capacity to forego egocentric self-interests that are obstacles to acting in a caring manner toward others. Self-surrender requires subordinating one's needs and desires to those of another. As noted in a previous chapter, self-surrender is a key component of Conn's theory of self-transcendence.

Concluding Note

This chapter briefly described the psychological domain of life and then shifted to the complex relationship between psychology and spirituality and psychology and the moral constructs of character and virtue. Psychology decisively dissociated itself from moral philosophy by taking a value-free stance, denigrating character and emphasizing personality in its most limited sense, and by eschewing its early focus on the scientific study of virtue. In place of virtue, psychology turned to cognitive-developmental models of moral development. The recent critique of a value-free psychology/psychotherapy, the retrieval of the moral dimension in psychotherapy, and the rise of "positive psychology's" retrieval of the empirical study of virtue were described as promising developments. Of particular note were Cloninger's theory of character and self-theory. Self-theory, which can be most useful in understanding the journey from the false self to the true self, was described in some detail. Finally, a taxonomy of self-capacities was presented. This taxonomy is a core component of the holistic and integrative model proposed in the next chapter.

6

An Integrative Model of Spiritual Direction and Pastoral Counseling

Contemporary trends suggest that there is considerable overlap among the moral, spiritual, and psychological domains, even though history reveals concerted efforts to separate the disciplines of moral theology and spiritual theology and psychology and moral philosophy. As noted in Chapters 3 and 4, moral and spiritual theology in the Christian tradition were a single discipline until they separated in the late sixteenth century. While several factors influenced this split, the result was that morality became the province of the commoners, while spirituality became the province of a small elite. Furthermore, morality became associated with rightness—instead of goodness, moral codes, sin, and living in the real world with daily duties and responsibilities—while spirituality was associated with holiness, altered states, contemplative prayer, and living an other worldly existence in a monastery or cloister. In short, the moral dimension is about goodness, while the spiritual dimension is about holiness. Everyone was expected to manifest goodness but only a few would achieve holiness. It should be noted that there was no such split between morality and spirituality in the Eastern religions.

Since the late 1960s there has been a gradual "reconciliation" among Western moral and spiritual theologies. Aspiring to both goodness and holiness is now viewed as possible both inside and outside the cloistered life. Nevertheless, consumerism, materialism, and unbridled individualism seem to be fueling a counter-cultural movement for the pursuit for spiritual development. Many contend that the spiritual journey requires that the spiritual and moral domains be pursued simultaneously and integrated with the other three dimensions of human experience.[1] It appears that many so called "New Age" spiritualities place a premium on the pursuit of holiness while downplaying the pursuit of goodness. Whether spiritual seekers pursue the journey of both goodness and holiness or only the holiness journey is and should be a basic consideration in spiritual direction and pastoral counseling.

Similarly, the discipline of psychology became separated from moral philosophy and from spiritual theology. Adopting a value-free stance was one way in which psychology distanced itself from moral philosophy. Denigrating the construct of character and disavowing its early focus on the empirical study of virtue were other strategies for separating from moral philosophy. At the outset of the twentieth century, academic psychology routinely studied religion and religious experiences. As noted in Chapter 5, just as psychology separated itself from moral philosophy it also decisively dissociated itself from the spiritual domain, particularly the study of religious and spiritual experiences. Nevertheless, there is considerable interest in "positive psychology," and the scientific study of virtue and its application to clinical and social concerns. Similarly, increasing interest in the study and application of transpersonal psychology, and particularly transpersonal psychotherapy, to both clinical and social concerns.

These trends toward an increasing rapprochement between moral theology and spirituality, moral philosophy and psychol-

[1] Ken Wilber, *Integral Psychology: Consciousness, Spirit, Psychology, Therapy: A Synthesis of Premodern, Modern and Postmodern Approaches* (Boston: Shambala, 1999); Thomas Keating, *Invitation to Love: The Way of Christian Contemplation* (New York: Continuum, 1998); Donald Gelpi, *The Conversion Experience: A Reflective Guide for RCIA Participants and Others* (New York: Paulist Press, 1998).

ogy, and between psychology and spirituality are heartening. A basic assumption of this book is that the spiritual, moral, and psychological domains are intimately related, and that the academic fields of spirituality, moral philosophy, moral theology, and psychology should encourage interdisciplinary study.

The following section further describes the relationship among the three domains by focusing on their relationship to the meta-domain of transformation.

The Meta-Domain of Transformation

What exactly is transformation? How is it related to the spiritual journey? What is its role in practical theology? How does it differ from self-transcendence? These and other questions are addressed in this section.

While the word transformation literally means a "change of form," it has a variety of meanings and applications in chemistry, economics, cultural anthropology, and consciousness studies. In the spiritual dimension of human experience, transformation is often used synonymously with conversion. Transformation is a common theme in the Christian Scriptures (i.e., John 16:13ff.; 1 Cor 15:51-52; 2 Pet 3:8ff.), as it is in other world religious and spiritual systems.[2] In the Christian tradition transformation includes both self-transformation and social transformation of the community and world under the reign of God.

This dual focus of transformation is central to practical theology. For instance, the mission statement of the Association of Graduate Programs in Ministry describes practical theology "as a mutually interpretive, critical and transforming conversation between the Christian tradition and contemporary experience . . . directed towards individual and social transformation in Christ."[3]

[2] Roger Walsh, *Essential Spirituality: The Seven Central Practices to Awaken Heart and Mind* (New York: Wiley, 1999).

[3] Quoted in Maureen O'Brien, "Practical Theology and Postmodern Religious Education," *Religious Education* 94 (1999) 316.

Transformation of consciousness is a more recent term used to describe changes impacting a person's somatic, intellectual, moral, socio-political, affective, and religious dimensions, which reflect a radically new self-understanding and world view. Transformation is described by Bernard Lonergan as the heart of conversion.[4] Conversion is a radical transformation in all the dimension of human experience: affective, moral, socio-political, intellectual, somatic, and religious dimensions. Since the spiritual dimension is central to all the other dimensions of human experience, transformation is essentially spiritual transformation. In short, the goal of the spiritual journey is transformation, and the purpose of prayer and other spiritual practices is to foster transformation.

Six dimensions of transformation are described in the following section. They articulate the meta-domain of transformation and serve as useful "markers" of progress on the spiritual journey. These six dimensions are: somatic, affective, intellectual, moral, sociopolitical, and religious/spiritual.

A Taxonomy of the Dimensions of Transformation

When transformation is used as a synonym for conversion, it means a turning away from something, and a subsequent turning toward something else. Donald Gelpi describes conversion as a turning from irresponsible behavior and a turning toward responsible behavior in some realm of experience.[5] His theology of conversion is based on the foundational theology of Lonergan[6] and the pragmatic philosophy of Charles Sanders Peirce. Because of the evangelistic connotations associated with conversion, the term transformation will be used instead of conversion

[4] Bernard Lonergan, *Method in Theology* (New York: Herder & Herder, 1972).

[5] Gelpi, *The Conversion Experience;* Donald Gelpi, *Committed Worship: A Sacramental Theology for Converting Christians,* vol. 1 (Collegeville: The Liturgical Press, 1993).

[6] Lonergan, *Method in Theology.*

throughout this book. In Lonergan's theology, there are two types of transformation: initial and ongoing. Initial transformation is defined as a preliminary shift from irresponsible to the responsible behavior in one or more dimensions of human experience, such as affective, moral, intellectual, or religious. Ongoing transformation refers to continuous, persisting development in all six dimensions. Transformation can also be thought of as integral, meaning that there is conscious commitment to living out these fundamental changes in all dimensions of life. Authentic transformation is described as movement beyond personal conversion to a living out of conversion in the sociopolitical world.[7] Gelpi and others have extended Lonergan's original formulation of intellectual, moral, and religious transformation to include the affective and sociopolitical dimensions. Len Sperry added the somatic dimension.[8]

Following is a brief description of these six dimensions of transformation.

The Religious/Spiritual Dimension of Transformation

Religious transformation, from a Christian perspective, challenges the individual to live for the one true God rather than mere idols. The goal of Christian transformation is a commitment to unconditionally finding God's will revealed in the person of Jesus, and his vision of the kingdom of God. Strategies for ongoing religious transformation include a regular prayer life, fasting, spiritual reading, and almsgiving.

The Affective Dimension of Transformation

Affective transformation means taking responsibility for one's emotional life with all its feelings, passions, and intentions.

[7] Gelpi, *The Conversion Experience,* 48.

[8] Len Sperry, "Spiritual Counseling and the Process of Conversion," *Journal of Christian Healing* 20:3 & 4 (1998); Len Sperry, "Leadership Dynamics: Character and Character Structure in Executives," *Consulting Psychology Journal* 49 (1997) 268–80.

Emotional healing requires the willingness to acknowledge and forgive past hurts. It presumes some measure of repentance, particularly the renouncement of the rage, fear, and guilt that separates the individual from God. As these negative affects are brought to healing in faith, individuals need to learn to own and express their positive affects and virtues, including love, friendship, compassion, sensitivity, and enthusiasm.

Ongoing affective transformation may require "sound spiritual direction and psychotherapy when necessary or helpful."[9] It demands a willingness to face one's own unconscious capacity for violence and destructive behaviors. Furthermore, forgiveness is essential in this type of ongoing conversion as it inaugurates a new level of conscious integration.

The Moral Dimension of Transformation

Moral transformation challenges the person to move from simple gratification of immediate personal needs to living by consistent principles of ethics and justice. Essential to this type of transformation is a formed conscience based on Christian moral principles. Subsequently, it involves the capacity to deal with moral dilemmas and challenges faced in everyday life. Ongoing transformation requires that the individual grasps the practical consequences of dedication to the common good as well as develop the requisite moral virtues. It also requires an increasing capacity to criticize false value systems that corrupt Christian conscience.

The Intellectual Dimension of Transformation

Intellectual transformation requires individuals to be able to understand and express their relationship to God and Jesus Christ in personally meaningful terms. It is not simply the capacity to recite a passage from Scripture or a catechism in response to theological questions. Intellectual transformation

[9] Gelpi, *Committed Worship*, 197.

also requires individuals to relentlessly pursue the truth and confront any form of false ideology and personal prejudices that rationalize sinful conduct. They should easily recognize beliefs that are inconsistent with Gospel values and eliminate self-deceit and self-righteousness. Furthermore, intellectual transformation "should inform every aspect of Christian growth and development such that individuals know and understand the dynamics of ongoing repentance and sound emotional growth in faith."[10]

In the process of ongoing intellectual transformation, they should have moved beyond mere knowledge of religious beliefs and tenets, and have come to a personal appropriation of these beliefs. It requires that individuals acquire a sufficient grasp of the theological issues and controversies surrounding their faith tradition to formulate their own position or response to these issues.

The Sociopolitical Dimension of Transformation

Religious, affective, intellectual, and moral transformation are considered types of "personal" transformation, which Gelpi notes is insufficient for authentic transformation. Authentic transformation requires that a person move and grow beyond personal transformation to sociopolitical transformation. This form of transformation de-privatizes personal transformation by confronting the individual with the world, that is the corporations, institutions, and vested interest groups that promote other value systems. Beyond personal moral principles, sociopolitical conversion generates its own moral principles. These include the "right of all persons to share in the good things of life, and the principles of legal, distributive and commutative justice."[11]

[10] Ibid., 199.
[11] Ibid., 45.

The Somatic Dimension of Transformation

Somatic refers to the human body, to body structure, and to bodily sensations, feelings—including sexual feelings—and memories. The body is the temple of the Holy Spirit (1 Cor 6:19), and is the physical expression or manifestation of an individual's spirit. Subsequently, when the body is injured, as in a motor vehicle accident or by a cerebrovascular stroke, this somatic expression may become distorted or limited. Likewise, if the individual's soul and spirit are pained, such as in mourning the loss of a close relative, a predictable somatic expression may be experienced as symptoms of grief.

Somatic transformation is primarily about wellness. Wellness is similar to, but not synonymous with, health, because wellness can coexist with chronic illness, disease, and even terminal illness. Individuals with a high level of somatic transformation can be expected to experience a high level of wellness irrespective of their health status.[12] To experience a high level of wellness, individuals need ongoing transformation in the somatic dimension. This includes the development of virtues such as temperance and physical fitness. It also includes preventive measures such as proper diet, exercise, and sleep, which can contribute effectively to one's degree of vitality, somatic wholeness, and transformation. However, preventive measures do not guarantee wellness, since wellness is not dependent on health status. Finally, individuals with a high level of somatic transformation are likely to have life-affirming attitudes toward their bodies—including sexuality—and will have integrated these attitudes into their philosophy of life.

Dynamics and Counter-Dynamics of Transformation

Furthermore, Gelpi describes the dynamics and counter-dynamics of transformation, where "dynamics" refers to the

[12] Len Sperry, "The Somatic Dimension in Healing Prayer and the Conversion Process," *Journal of Christian Healing* 21:3 & 4 (1999) 47–62.

way in which the different forms of transformation mutually reinforce one another and "counter-dynamics" refer to the ways in which the absence of transformation in one dimension tends to undermine and subvert transformation in another dimension.[13] He then describes these seven dynamics. Affective transformation animates the other forms of conversion. Similarly, intellectual transformation informs and orders the other forms. Personal moral transformation helps orient the other four forms toward principles that make ultimate and absolute ethical claims. Affective, intellectual, personal moral, and religious transformation help authenticate sociopolitical conversion by providing norms for judging the justice or injustice of human institutions. Initial Christian religious transformation mediates between affective transformation and the two forms of moral transformation. In addition, "ongoing Christian transformation transvalues the other four forms of transformation."[14] Finally, somatic transformation energizes and vitalizes all other forms of transformation, while at the same time visibly reflecting one's overall level of wellness.

Self-Transcendence and Transformation

But what about self-transcendence and its relation to transformation? Self-transcendence has been described as the most basic human drive, which is the radical desire for a relationship with God. That is,

> the fundamental desire of the self is to transcend itself in relationship: to the world, to other, to God. But only a developed powerful self has the strength to realize significant transcendence. . . . The desire to be a self and to reach out beyond the self must be understood together. . . . This dual desire of the human heart is . . . self-transcendence.[15]

[13] Gelpi, *The Conversion Experience.*

[14] Ibid., 42–3.

[15] Walter Conn, *The Desiring Self: Rooting Pastoral Counseling and Spiritual Direction in Self-Transcendence* (New York: Paulist Press, 1998) 5.

Although Walter Conn describes self-transcendence as having both a theological and psychological basis, his articulation of self-transcendence is heavily dependent on theoretical constructs from both object-relations and self-psychology.

Is self-transcendence the same as self-actualization or self-fulfillment? Citing Vicktor Frankl,[16] Conn contends that an individual is actualized or fulfilled only to the extent to which that person is committed to life's meaning: "Self-actualization cannot be attained if it is made an end in itself, but only as a side effect of self-transcendence."[17] Furthermore, Conn suggests that self-transcendence is related to conversion and, thus, to transformation by describing the dimensions of conversion as "special instances of self-transcendence that transform our lives in fundamental ways."[18] The position espoused in this book is that the dimensions of conversion, i.e., the six dimensions of transformation, reflect the transformation meta-domain of life, rather than being simply "special instances" of self-transcendence as described by Conn. Furthermore, this book views self-transcendence as only one element of transformation—albeit an important element. Finally, transformation, rather than self-transcendence, is the common designation used in the great world religious and spiritual traditions. In other words, as used in this book, transformation is inclusive of self-transcendence.

An Integrative Model: Spiritual Practices, Virtues, Self-Capacities and Transformation

In Chapter 2 the relationship of the dimensions of transformation to the three domains of life was described. The holistic, integrative model described here further extends that discussion. The proposed model correlates and specifies relationships among the taxonomies of self-capacities, spiritual

[16] Vicktor Frankl, *The Doctor and the Soul: From Psychotherapy to Logotherapy* (New York: Knopf, 1955).

[17] Conn, *The Desiring Self,* 175.

[18] Ibid., 36.

practices, and virtues with the six dimensions of transformation. Each of these taxonomies is briefly described and the interrelationships among the taxonomies and the dimensions of transformation are briefly noted.

Transformation

Across the major religious and spiritual traditions, transformation is considered the endpoint or outcome of the spiritual journey. As noted earlier, transformation is a considerably broader construct than self-transcendence. In the Christian tradition transformation includes both self-transformation, or conversion, as well as social transformation of the community and world under the reign of God. Transformation is a process of change into a mature relationship with God that has repercussions for human relationships and human actions. As such, it involves grace. According to William Spohn, "transformation is primarily attributed to the grace of God, but it also involves human cooperation."[19]

The taxonomy selected for transformation is adapted from the works of Lonergan,[20] Gelpi,[21] and Sperry,[22] and reflects both transformation of self and community. This taxonomy involves the six dimensions of transformation: somatic, affective, religious/spiritual, moral, intellectual, and sociopolitical. It is noteworthy that Howard Clinebell describes six nearly identical dimensions in his highly regarded "revised model" of pastoral counseling and, by extension, spiritual direction.[23]

As used in this book, the taxonomy of the dimensions of transformation articulates the meta-domain of transformation,

[19] William Spohn, *Go and Do Likewise: Jesus and Ethics* (New York: Continuum, 2000) 40.

[20] Lonergan, *Method in Theology.*

[21] Gelpi, *The Conversion Experience.*

[22] Sperry, "Spiritual Counseling and the Process of Conversion"; Sperry, "The Somatic Dimension in Healing Prayer and the Conversion Process."

[23] Howard Clinebell, *Basic Types of Pastoral Care and Counseling,* rev. ed. (Nashville: Abingdon, 1984).

and can be thought of as outcomes or "markers" of the three other taxonomies which articulate the moral, spiritual, and psychological domains. Clinically, such "markers" are most useful in assessing a client's overall level of life functioning, particularly in the context of spiritual direction and pastoral counseling. Table 6.1 briefly describes these dimensions of transformation.

Table 6.1: Types and Descriptions of Dimensions of Transformation

Dimensions of Transformation	**Description of the Dimensions**
Somatic	Refers to body structure, bodily sensations, and memories. It is primarily about achieving and maintaining a relatively high degree of wellness despite a disability, disease, or terminal illness.
Affective	Involves taking responsibility for one's emotional well-being. It requires the forgiveness of past hurts and the replacement of anger, fear, and guilt with love, compassion, sensitivity, and enthusiasm.
Religious/Spiritual	Challenges the individual to live for the one true God instead of idols such as reputation, wealth, and power. The goal is a commitment to unconditionally seek God's will and vision of the kingdom of God.
Moral	Challenges the person to move from simple gratification of immediate personal needs to living by consistent principles of ethics and justice. It involves the capacity to deal with moral dilemmas and challenges faced in everyday life and to criticize false value systems that corrupt Christian conscience.
Intellectual	Involves the pursuit of the truth amidst ideologies and personal prejudices that rationalize sinful conduct. Beyond a knowledge of religious beliefs and tenets, it requires a sufficient critical grasp of theological issues and controversies in order to respond effectively.
Sociopolitical	Involves moving beyond self-transformation to bring about the reign of God in one's community and the world. It requires a commitment to challenging corporations, institutions, and vested interest groups that promote other value systems.

Virtues

The moral domain of life is quite broad and includes character, virtue, sin, moral precepts, and asceticism to name a few. Traditionally, moral theology has emphasized character since it provides orientation and direction to life. The time honored maxim "plant an act, reap a habit; plant a habit, reap a virtue; plant a virtue, reap a character; plant a character, reap a destiny" makes this point and indicates the requisites of character.[24] Since character emerges from a constellation of an individual's virtues and vices, virtue was selected as the basis for developing a taxonomy of the moral domain that would be germane to the practice of spiritual direction and pastoral counseling. Unlike psychological constructs such as personality and self, which focus primarily on the individual, character is a construct which focuses on the individual's relationship and responsibility to both self and community. Thus, character and virtue are principally social rather than personal constructs. The taxonomy was derived from the listings or "taxonomies" of James Keenan[25] and Bernard Haring.[26] Selection was based on the extent of correlation with the six dimensions of transformation. The following virtues are ordered in this taxonomy: temperance, physical fitness, compassion, self-care, charity, holiness, trustworthiness, fidelity, prudence, and justice. Table 6.2 provides capsule descriptions of these virtues.

[24] Richard McBrien, *Catholicism*, new ed. (San Francisco: HarperSanFrancisco, 1994) 926.

[25] James Keenan, *Virtues for Ordinary Christians* (Kansas City, Mo.: Sheed & Ward, 1996).

[26] Bernard Haring, *The Virtues of an Authentic Life: A Celebration of Christian Maturity* (Liguori, Mo.: Liguori, 1997).

Table 6.2: Types and Descriptions of Virtues

Virtue	Brief Definition
Temperance	Moderates the attraction of pleasures and balances one's desire to achieve good through food, drink, or other sensual pleasures.
Physical fitness	Taking responsibility for one's own physical health and well-being
Compassion	Enables one to understand and respond with caring and concern to the other's frame of reference.
Self-Care	Ensures taking responsibility for one's own psychological health and well-being, which is the expression of the virtue of self-love.
Charity	A freely given gift of God which unites us to God and enables us to curb our self-centeredness and reach out to others.
Holiness	Enables one to mediate the presence of God in one's environment.
Trustworthiness	Enables one to relate to others with honesty, fairness, truthfulness, loyalty, dependability, and humility.
Fidelity	Ensures treating those to whom one is closely related, i.e., friends, spouse, children, community members, etc., with special care and concern.
Prudence	Disposes an individual to discern true good in circumstances and to choose the right means of achieving it.
Justice	Ensures treating others equally and fairly, as well as about recognizing unfairness and inequality in the world around us.
Fortitude/courage	Ensures firmness in difficulties, i.e., facing fears, trials, sacrificing for a just cause, and constancy in the pursuit of the good.

Spiritual Practices

While the spiritual domain of life is also very broad, the actual practice of spiritual disciplines or techniques is one of the most personal and tangible aspects of spirituality. The challenge was to find or develop a taxonomy of such spiritual practices. Roger Walsh has described seven classes or categories of spiritual practices which he derived from the major spiritual and religious traditions.[27] These classes of spiritual practices correlated highly with the six dimensions of transformation, and appear to be germane to the practice of spiritual direction and pastoral counseling. The resulting taxonomy also correlates with the taxonomy of virtues. The classes of spiritual practices are: transforming cravings, healing the heart and learning to love, awakening spiritual vision, developing wisdom and understanding, and expressing spirit in service. Table 6.3 provides examples of these practices.

Table 6.3: Types and Examples of Spiritual Practices

Types of Spiritual Practices	**Examples of Spiritual Techniques and Methods**
transforming cravings and redirecting desires	fasting; single pointed attention; custody of the senses; exercise regimen; commitment to simple living
healing the heart and learning to love	forgiveness; reconciliation; inner healing work; reframing fear, hurt, and anger
awakening spiritual vision	centering prayer; meditation; mantra; community worship; mindfulness in eating, walking, listening, and speech
living ethically	practicing right actions, giving up gossip, practicing truthfulness, confession and making amends
developing wisdom and spiritual understanding	spiritual reading, committing time to silence and solitude, recognizing the sacred in all things
expressing spirit in service	almsgiving, tithing, voting regularly, involvement in volunteer activities, advocating justice for the poor, etc.

[27] Walsh, *Essential Spirituality.*

Self-Capacities

The psychological domain, especially when viewed from a spiritual perspective, has traditionally emphasized self-theory. This emphasis, or overemphasis, on self-theory has been the source of considerable criticism and concern. Nevertheless, the construct of self is intimately related to the construct of character, and both can be conceptualized as representing two sides of a coin. The most tangible aspect of self is self-capacity. Self-capacities are defined as requisite abilities that are essential for adequate personal functioning and adequate functioning in relationships and in the community. James Masterson described ten such capacities derived from research in the areas of object relations and self-psychology.[28] These were supplemented with three additional self-capacities in order to establish a taxonomy that correlated with the dimensions of transformation and the taxonomies of virtues and spiritual practices. These self-capacities are: self-activation, self-mastery, self-acknowledgment, spontaneity, self-soothing, intimacy, self-continuity, creativity, autonomy, self-surrender, commitment, critical reflection, and critical social consciousness. Table 6.4 briefly provides capsule descriptions of these self-capacities.

Table 6.4: Types and Descriptions of Self-Capacities

Self-Capacity	**Brief Description**
Self-Activation	Capacity to identify one's unique individuality, goals, and wishes, and then to be assertive in expressing and achieving them.
Self-Mastery	Capacity to achieve a balance of pleasure and self-control over needs, desires, wishes, and cravings.
Self-Acknowledgment	Capacity to renew belief in one's own worthiness and to acknowledge having effectively coped with a crisis or concern.

[28] James Masterson, *The Real Self: A Developmental Self and Object Relations Approach* (New York: Brunner/Mazel, 1985); James Masterson, *The Personality Disorders* (Phoenix: Zieg/Tucker, 2000).

Table 6.4: (Cont.)

Spontaneity	Capacity to experience a wide range of feelings appropriately, deeply, and without blocking or deadening their impact.
Self-Soothing	Capacity to limit, minimize, and soothe painful affects without recourse to emotional numbing, depersonalization, or derealization.
Intimacy	Capacity to express the self fully in a close relationship with minimal anxiety or fears of rejection.
Self-Continuity	Capacity to recognize and to acknowledge that the inner self persists and is continuous through space and over time.
Creativity	Capacity to use the self to replace old familiar patterns with new, unique, and different patterns.
Autonomy	Capacity to regulate self-esteem and to be alone with minimal fear of abandonment or engulfment.
Self-Surrender	Capacity to forego self-interests that are obstacles to being caring and compassionate.
Commitment	Capacity to commit to a personal, community, or career goal or to a relationship and then to persevere in that commitment.
Critical Reflection	Capacity to objectively analyze ideas, ideologies, and situations and related underlying assumptions.
Critical Social Consciousness	Capacity to analyze social situations in terms of ethical and moral assumptions and consequences.

Table 6.5 depicts these four taxonomies—the three domains of moral, spiritual, and psychological—and their articulation for the six dimensions of transformation, spiritual practices, and virtues.

Table 6.5: Correlation of Aspects of the Moral, Spiritual, and Psychological Domains to Transformation

Moral Domain	Spiritual Domain	Psychological Domain	Transformation Meta-Domain
Virtues	*Spiritual Practices*	*Self-Capacities*	*Dimensions of Transformation*
temperance, physical fitness	transforming cravings	self-activation, self-mastery	Somatic
compassion, self-care	healing the heart, learning to love	self-acknowledgment, spontaneity, self-soothing, intimacy, self-continuity, creativity, autonomy	Affective
charity, holiness	awakening spiritual vision	self-surrender (autonomy)	Religious/ Spiritual
trustworthiness, fidelity	living ethically	commitment (intimacy)	Moral
prudence	developing wisdom and understanding	critical reflection	Intellectual
justice, fortitude/ courage	expressing spirit in service	social consciousness	Sociopolitical

Relationship of Transformation and Virtue

Virtues can be defined as "developed dispositions that realize particular dimensions of our lives so that we live and act rightly."[29] Dispositions, dimensions, and acting rightly are three characteristics emphasized in this definition. First, unlike spirit-

[29] James Keenan, "How Catholic Are the Virtues?" *America* 176 (June 7, 1997) 17.

ual practices which are techniques and activities, or self-capacities which are abilities and skills, virtues are the development of dispositions. Dispositions are inclinations or innate qualities. Virtues are dispositions which must be developed by practice, i.e., repeatedly acting courageously results in the virtue of courage. If not developed, a disposition will atrophy. Second, virtues help us realize the six dimensions of transformation: somatic, affective, moral, intellectual, religious/spiritual, and sociopolitical. Third, when compared with self-capacities and spiritual practices, "acting rightly" is a characteristic unique to virtue. It reflects a norm or standard of rightness. Furthermore, there are two classes of virtue: acquired virtues (i.e., those attained by practice) and infused virtues (i.e., those given as gifts from God).

More specifically, how do virtues facilitate transformation? Keenan notes that "virtues, then, transform our dispositions. The acquired virtues transform a person by prudential guidance into right exercises that eventually shape and rightly order a person's inclinations or dispositions; the infused virtues transform by God's working on our own disposition."[30]

The relationship between the dimensions of transformation and virtue is illustrated in Table 6.6.

Table 6.6: Dimensions of Transformation and Virtues

Dimensions of Transformation	**Related Virtues**
Religious/Christian	Charity, Holiness
Intellectual	Prudence
Affective	Self-Care, Compassion
Moral	Fidelity, Trustworthiness
Sociopolitical	Justice
Somatic	Temperance; Physical Fitness

[30] Ibid.

Relationship of Transformation and Self-Capacities

As noted above, self-capacities are abilities and skills rather than dispositions or activities. They are instinctual or inherent abilities that appear to be "hardwired" in the central nervous system. Whether these capabilities are actualized and expressed depends, in large part, on early environment experiences, such as being exposed to supportive parents and caretakers who both model such capacities and expect and challenge the child to express these capabilities. Thus, given a reasonably supportive environment infants and young children who experience some degree of distress will be observed to utilize the self-capacity of self-soothing when no one else is available to soothe them.

How do self-capacities facilitate transformation? Self-capacities function as the substrate or requisites for the development of the healthy self. To the extent to which there is sufficient effort and the expectation that a given self-capacity be actualized and expressed, it is likely that a specific dimension of transformation will result. For example, critical reflection is the requisite self-capacity for developing the intellectual dimension of transformation. Furthermore, the development of this dimension can be facilitated by practice of the virtue of prudence and spiritual practices that develop wisdom and understanding, such as spiritual reading, life review, corrective visualization, etc.

The relationship between the dimensions of transformation and self-capacities is illustrated in Table 6.7.

Table 6.7: Dimensions of Transformation and Self-Capacities

Dimensions of Transformation	Related Self-Capacities
Religious/Christian	Autonomy, Self-Surrender
Intellectual	Critical Reflection
Affective	Intimacy, Spontaneity, Self-Soothing
Moral	Commitment
Sociopolitical	Critical Social Consciousness
Somatic	Self-Activation, Self-Maintenance

Relationship of Transformation and Spiritual Practices

As noted earlier, spiritual practices are techniques and activities rather than dispositions or abilities. They are techniques and activities which strengthen and support the seeker on the spiritual journey. Spiritual writers view spiritual practices as means to growth and transformation, rather than ends in themselves. For instance, St. John Caspian says that "Fasting, vigils, the study of scripture, renouncing possessions and the world—these are the means not the end. Perfection is not found in them, but through them. It is pointless to boast about such practices when we have not achieved the love of God and our fellow humans."[31]

What is the relationship between spiritual practices and transformation? Spiritual practices "are about transforming our habitual states of mind and awakening our new spiritual consciousness."[32] For example, activities such as fasting and custody of the senses are age-old spiritual practices of transforming cravings that facilitate transformation of the somatic dimension. The relationship between the dimensions of transformation and spiritual practices is illustrated in Table 6.8.

Table 6.8: Dimensions of Transformation and Spiritual Practices

Dimensions of Transformation	**Related Spiritual Practices**
Religious/Christian	Awakening Spiritual Vision
Intellectual	Developing Wisdom and Understanding
Affective	Healing the Heart, Learning to Love
Moral	Living Ethically
Sociopolitical	Expressing Spirit in Service
Somatic	Transforming Cravings

[31] St. John Caspian as quoted in Timothy Freke, *Encyclopedia of Spirituality* (New York: Sterling Publishing, 2000) 56.

[32] Ibid., 54.

To recap, the proposed model highlights and describes virtues, spiritual practices, and self-capacities. As "markers" or measures of clinical reality, virtues, spiritual practices, and self-capacities can be assessed and serve as the basis for the session-to-session practice of pastoral counseling and spiritual direction.

The Value and Utility of the Integrative Model

The integrative model is centered on the dimensions of transformation and the three taxonomies. The hope was that this model would have considerable value and clinical utility to assess, select goals and focus, and plan interventions for the course of spiritual direction and pastoral counseling. This section describes both the conceptual value and the practical value of this integrative model.

Conceptual Value

Conceptually, the value of the integrative model can be demonstrated. First, the integrative model addresses the criticism that most current theories underlying the practice of spiritual direction and pastoral counseling are essentially reductionistic in that they "reduce" the life concerns of clients and directees to psychological and/or spiritual constructs, and avoid the moral domain. The integrative model, however, encompasses the moral domain as well as the spiritual and psychological domains. Furthermore, the integrative model conceptualizes spiritual development, psychological development, and moral development as separate lines of development that can and do overlap but cannot be reduced to a single line of development.

Second, the integrative model addresses the criticism that most current theories are over-reliant on psychological constructs and tend to foster individualism and/or spiritual narcissism. The integrative model, however, emphasizes constructs from all three life domains, i.e., the moral, the spiritual, as well as the psychological. Not surprisingly, the individualistic perspective of psychological theories and constructs emphasizes the goal of self-transformation. On the other hand, the integrative model emphasizes and advocates for social transformation in addition to self-transformation. Furthermore, the integrative model articulates the process of self and social transformation in terms of virtues, spiritual practices, and the self-capacities.

Practical Value

Practically, the value of the integrative model can be demonstrated. First, the integrative model facilitates a holistic assessment of the clients' or directees' levels of spiritual, moral, and psychological functioning, the dimensions of transformation, as well as of virtues, spiritual practices, and self-capacities.

Second, the integrative model facilitates the process of selecting a focus and goals for the course of spiritual direction or pastoral counseling based on deficits or developmental delays noted in the holistic assessment. Third, the integrative model facilitates the process of planning interventions and monitoring changes in the course of spiritual direction or pastoral counseling.

Finally, the integrated model also has the potential for ensuring that the practice of spiritual direction and pastoral counseling does not become overly parochial. This means that it is unlikely that utilizing the integrative model in spiritual direction will limit its focus primarily to the religious and moral dimensions of transformation, nor that utilizing the integrative model in pastoral counseling will limit its focus primarily to the affective dimension of transformation.

For most individuals on the spiritual journey, personal development and spiritual growth do not proceed at the same rate on all five dimensions. Often one or more dimensions will lag behind the others. Presumably, discerning spiritual directors and pastoral counselors will be able to recognize these developmental lags in their holistic assessment and address them with clients.

Utilizing the Integrative Model in the Practice of Spiritual Direction and Pastoral Counseling

The integrative model can be effectively utilized as a framework for guiding the course of spiritual direction or pastoral counseling, including specifying a focus and targeted goals as well as for establishing an intervention plan. Using the model, particularly the dimensions of transformation, also sensitizes the spiritual director and pastoral counselor to the fact that ongoing transformation is multi-faceted, rather than single-faceted, such as focusing primarily on the affective domain in pastoral counseling or on the religious/spiritual dimension in spiritual direction.

Protocol and Practice Guidelines

A simple protocol, consisting of a set of practice guidelines, for utilizing the integrative model in the practice of pastoral counseling and spiritual direction is described in this section. These guidelines provide pastoral counselors and spiritual directors strategies for facilitating process and outcomes. Seven steps or strategies are involved:

1. Establish a relationship of mutuality. Through the use of active listening, respect, and unconditional positive regard, engage the directee or client in the counseling or direction process. Elicit the directee's or client's concerns and expectations for spiritual direction or pastoral counseling, and commitment to the process.

2. Begin an assessment of the dimensions of transformation. Involve the directee or client in the assessment of the six dimensions. This orients the directee or client to transformation—both self-transformation and social transformation—as the goal of the spiritual direction and pastoral counseling. Together estimate the level of functioning for each dimension.

3. Assess levels of virtues, spiritual practices, and self-capacities. Note the absence of virtue and spiritual practices for the dimensions of transformation with low levels of functioning. Some counselors and directors may find it useful to share the descriptions of the self-capacities with clients or directees and seek their input. It may be necessary to extend this assessment end beyond the initial meeting or session. The purpose is to identify any developmental lags or deficits for each dimension of transformation.

4. Highlight deficits in virtue, spiritual practices, self-capacities. Based on this assessment of the dimensions of transformation, self-capacities, virtues, and spiritual practices, highlight or underline those dimensions of transformation with deficits or lags, as well as corresponding self-capacities, virtues, and self-practices. These will become the focus of the counseling or spiritual direction.

5. Specify a plan. In collaboration with the directee or client, decide on a plan for the course of counseling or direction. The plan will include both focus and goals. The focus may be the client's or directee's presenting concern or expectation for the outcome of counseling or direction, or it may emerge from Step 4, analysis of the matrix. Then specify and prioritize goals which are the end points or outcomes of the focus. This may include virtues to be cultivated and practiced, a specific spiritual practice, or therapeutic goals such as symptom reduction, increased assertiveness, etc. Finally, indicate specific ways of achieving these goals such as prayer methods, therapeutic interventions, or referral for goals beyond one's competence and scope of practice.

6. Implement the plan. Implement the plan utilizing methods or interventions targeted to the focus and goals.

7. Assess and monitor progress. Targeted "markers" of progress may be helpful in determining growth or change. For example, "the number of days per week and time spent per day in centering prayer," or "reduction or absence of insomnia and anxiety symptoms when alone or feeling conflicted." Again, collaborating with the directee or client about choosing markers and monitoring progress encourages commitment and involvement.

Examples and Applications

How would this protocol actually be used? For example, consider the situation in which a pastoral counselor assesses all dimensions of transformation and finds some deficits in the affective dimension. The counselor would then assess for the presence or absence of requisite self-capacities (e.g., low in autonomy), the extent to which the clients has mastered requisite spiritual practices in this dimension (e.g., deficit in healing the heart), as well as the extent of requisite virtues (e.g., low in self-care). Initially or sometime later, the counselor could then focus on increasing autonomy, emotional healing, and the acquisition of the virtue of self-care. Intervention strategies would then be considered, including the prospect of referral for areas outside the counselor's area of competence. Strategies and methods as well as time frames could then be discussed and established with the client. In this example, these might include focusing on forgiveness regarding certain circumstances or relationships, prescribing specific spiritual practices to facilitate healing the heart, the virtue of self-care, and possibly a formal psychotherapeutic focus on an emotion such as anger.

If the client lags on the intellectual dimension, the counselor or director must assess the nature of this lag. If the individual client has considerable theological illiteracy, specified readings or formal instruction might be suggested. If the client has yet to integrate family, career, and finances within the context of a balanced philosophy of life, these may be an appropriate counseling goal.

If the client lags on the sociopolitical dimension, an assessment of the nature of this lag is needed. This, of course, is a two-pronged dimension with both a personal component (e.g., resisting prejudices, overcoming the urge to security and refusing personal luxury at the expense of the poor) and a political component (e.g., making some commitment or dedication to a social justice cause). Accordingly, some counselors and directors may be uncomfortable with the thought of mixing the personal and therapeutic with the social, or the religious with the political. And that is understandable, given the training and values of most pastoral counselors, especially those influenced by psychological and psychoanalytic theories. On the other hand, pastoral counselors trained in a more anthropological and cross-cultural model will tend to be more sensitive to the sociopolitical dimension of transformation. Whatever one's training or political persuasion, the Gospel message does address both personal sin and sociopolitical sin. Accordingly, transformation requires the sociopolitical dimension.

Concluding Note

It was noted that the meta-domain of transformation subsumes the moral, psychological, and spiritual domains of life. Six dimensions of transformation were described: the intellectual, affective, moral, sociopolitical, religious, and somatic.

A holistic, integrative model for the practice of pastoral counselors and spiritual direction was presented. It was derived from the disciplines of spiritual theology, moral theology, and psychology and their corresponding spiritual, moral, and psychological domains. From the discussion of the spiritual dimension both spirituality and spiritual practices were highlighted. From the discussion of the moral dimension both character and virtues were highlighted, while the discussion of the psychological dimension highlighted self-theory and self-capacities. A case was made that the constructs of self-capacities, spiritual practices, and virtues, as they relate to corresponding dimensions of transformation, are essential elements for an integrative approach to the practice of pastoral counseling and spiritual direction.

Finally, the clinical value of the integrative model was demonstrated in assessing client needs and functioning, selecting goals and a focus, planning interventions, and monitoring progress throughout the course of spiritual direction and pastoral counseling. Chapters 7 and 8 will further illustrate the value and clinical utility of this integrated model with two full-length case studies.

7

An Integrative Approach to Spiritual Direction: A Case Study

Case material can reveal the theoretical premises and practice patterns of the spiritual directors. A spiritual direction case is offered here to illustrate how to apply the integrative model to a relatively common case. It also shows the value and clinical utility of this model. To safeguard confidentiality actual case material will not be provided. Instead, the case material presented here represents a composite of cases from my clinical and supervisory experience.

Spiritual Direction with Jane S.

Initial Presentation

Jane S., forty-eight years old, has been the director of religious education at a mid-sized Presbyterian parish for nine years. She is married with three children and four grandchildren. Her youngest child has recently left home for college and Jane now feels she has "a little more time to be serious about my spiritual life." This is her first experience with spiritual direction and she is eager to "make up for lost time." As director of religious education she had occasionally recommended spiritual direction to those completing the program, and now felt it was time to abide by her own recommendation. For the past several years her religious practices have included daily formula prayer, occasional Scripture reading—usually related to her teaching responsibilities—and Sunday worship services. She had once tried to meditate but had given up after about a week or so. Her image of God is described as "like a caring grandmother."

Personality and Systems Dynamics

Jane is the older of two female siblings. Her younger sister is a CPA who has never married and apparently has little "religious sentiment," according to Jane. Both parents are alive and relatively healthy and live in the same city. Her parents were reportedly active in their church, and her mother was also a religious education director for many years. Jane believes they "provided a real living example of what it means to be a Christian." She attended the local Presbyterian college, graduating with a B.A. in religious education. She married her high school sweetheart soon after college graduation and reports being reasonably happy in her twenty-three-year marriage to Willard. She reports that he has been supportive of her decision to begin spiritual direction, just as he was when she went back to school for a masters degree in religious education five years ago.

She indicates that she has been blessed with excellent health, although following the birth of her third child she received short-term treatment consisting of medication and counseling for postpartum depression. Other personal or family history of mental health or substance abuse treatment is denied. Jane reported that she has found her roles as mother, wife, and religious education director to be gratifying, though "occasionally challenging."

When asked to elaborate on being challenged, she mentions the newly assigned pastor who "seems to be running a reign of terror" among parish staff. It seems that following the untimely death of the previous pastor a year ago, there was a delay of six months before the pastorate was filled. Soon after arriving at his new assignment the new pastor fired the full-time music director of nine years for "insubordination." Recently, he had "dismissed" two of Jane's volunteer teaching staff because they apparently questioned a comment he had made. She felt quite badly about losing them since, besides being her best catechists, they are also close personal friends. When she tried to talk to the pastor about reinstating the two, she was told "never to question my judgment if you want to stay here." Three weeks ago, one of her volunteer teachers had complained that the pastor had made threatening comments to her and that she had smelled alcohol on his breath. The volunteer wanted to know what the director would do. Jane was not sure what she might do, particularly since she felt so intimidated by the pastor and really didn't want to lose her job. Although she recognized that as a member of the pastoral team she had some responsibility for these matters, she politely declined to discuss them in spiritual direction saying: "I'm just here to work on my prayer life."

Psychospiritual Dynamics

From a psychospiritual perspective, Jane would be considered a good candidate for spiritual direction. She appears to be a reasonably mature individual—psychologically and spiritually—who has a good social support system, no obvious history of religious or spiritual abuse or baggage, appropriate motivation, as well as the commitment to embark on a deeper spiritual journey. Her personality appears to be that of a pleaser and reconciler. Her commitment to her current spiritual practices and her positive image of God are additional strengths. Her expectations of spiritual direction is to deepen her prayer life.

A Reductionistic Approach to the Case

Unlike psychotherapists and pastoral counselors, who typically specify or imply a case formulation which explains the cause of the client's concerns or distress, spiritual directors traditionally do not specify such a case formulation or a formal treatment plan. Nevertheless, the course of spiritual direction usually follows a specified or implied focus and goal(s). Reductionistic approaches specify or imply a focus and goals which are limited to the spiritual and/or psychological domains and typically exclude the moral domain. To the extent to which spiritual direction is limited to one or two of the life domains it would be considered a reductionistic approach.

Proposed Focus and Goals of Spiritual Direction

What might be a reasonable focus and goals of spiritual direction? In light of Jane's expectations for spiritual direction, i.e., "to work on my prayer life," and her overall level of moderate to high functioning it doesn't appear that much if any focus on past or current psychotherapeutic issues is indicated. Thus, a reasonable focus and goals might be to concentrate primarily on deepening her prayer life and secondarily on increasing autonomy, i.e., becoming more assertive with her co-workers and boss. At least, this may be a spiritual director's first impression.

Addenda

In terms of psychological types, Jane resembled a Two on the Enneagram. While many spiritual directors would not likely assess their clients with regard to various developmental stages, i.e., faith, self, and spiritual development, the following developmental stage profile of Jane is given to provide an even fuller portrait of her spiritual capacities and functioning. In terms of Fowler's stages of faith schema, Jane would be assessed at the conjunctive stage of faith, meaning that she appears to be capable of integrating her religious and spiritual beliefs into the self.[1] With regard to Robert Kegan's stages of self-development,

[1] James Fowler, *Stages of Faith: The Psychology of Human Development and the Quest for Meaning* (San Francisco: HarperSanFrancisco, 1995).

she appears to be moving toward the inter-individual stage, wherein she would be expected to have achieved the capacity to control self by acting autonomously and independently, while at the same time being able to freely choose to be dependent on others.[2] This capacity to combine both independence and dependence is called interdependence. In addition, at this stage Jane should find it increasingly easier to tolerate inner conflicts and relate to others with genuine intimacy. She also appears to be moving toward Daniel Helminiak's compassionate stage of spiritual development, wherein commitment to life and relationships is more realistic, nuanced, and supported by deeply felt emotion.[3] Finally, it appears that Jane has a moderately high degree of self-transcendence, reasonably balancing autonomy and self-surrender, according to Walter Conn's theory.[4]

Reservations About the Reductionistic Approach to the Case

Beyond these first impressions, a number of observations can be made and concerns need to be expressed.

(1) Although the case describes a psychospiritual formulation based on several elements that are currently in vogue, i.e., image of God, prayer style, religious and spiritual practices, as well as stages of self, faith, and spiritual development, along with an indication of level of self-transcendence, these markers do not easily translate into targeted treatment goals or a plan of intervention. While spiritual practices can be a tangible marker to assess and monitor change, knowledge of the client's stages of faith, self, and spiritual development do not seem to have any obvious value to a spiritual director in a particular session.

[2] Robert Kegan, *The Evolving Self: Problem and Process in Human Development* (Cambridge, Mass.: Harvard University Press, 1983).

[3] Daniel Helminiak, *Spiritual Development: An Interdisciplinary Study* (Chicago: Loyola University Press, 1987).

[4] Walter Conn, *The Desiring Self: Rooting Pastoral Counseling and Spiritual Direction in Self-Transcendence* (New York: Paulist Press, 1998).

(2) The goal of focusing on prayer and meditation is reasonable, but how specifically can this focus be operationalized? How exactly should the spiritual director proceed? What prayer or meditation method should be recommended or taught, and what is the rationale for the recommendation? Also, the goal of "increasing her autonomy" is somewhat vague and problematic. It is not indicated how this would be accomplished, and efforts to urge her to be more assertive may be unrealistic given her previous pattern of pleasing others and being self-effacing. In fact, following the plan to act more assertively with her pastor might actually lead to her being fired.

(3) Is her image of God really appropriate and healthy for her? An image of God as "like a caring grandmother" seems positive and life-giving compared to viewing God as an exacting judge or tyrant. However, might imaging God only in this fashion effectively restrain Jane from acting responsibly and courageously in situations that reasonably demand her to be more than kind and caring, such as being assertive and seeking justice in her administrative role in the parish? Might she do well to foster another image of God as just and courageous, as well as caring and loving?

(4) What about the moral issues? Because Jane did not specifically ask or agree that work-related issues, particularly the pastor's abusive behavior, become a focus of direction, should the spiritual director refrain from broaching the matter? Because Jane did not view the matter of her responsibility regarding the pastor's seemingly abusive behavior a focus of spiritual direction, the spiritual director did not make it a focus of their work together. That is because many training programs and supervisors advocate the position that matters are not to be addressed unless the client initiates them. And while there may be a few exceptions, e.g., threats to seriously harm another and suicide gestures, many spiritual directors and pastoral counselors would adhere to this practice guideline. The question that probably was not addressed is: Can Jane become more transformed if she fails to act courageously when she probably should?

(5) Finally, is the goal of increased transformation possible if Jane silently avoids dealing with difficult situations, particularly the impact of the pastor's seemingly abusive and inappropriate behavior on her staff and on the parish?

In many respects the aforementioned psychospiritual formulation and goals and plan for the course of spiritual dimension raise more questions and considerations than they answer. These questions and considerations seem to strike to the heart of the foundation theory or theories that inform the way in which this spiritual director has conceptualized and formulated this case. These questions and considerations also suggest that the practice guidelines and protocols that spiritual directors are traditionally taught and expected to utilize, i.e., minimizing, referring or refusing to deal with moral concerns, are non-responsive to client need and may be non-defensible. As the following discussion demonstrates, all five of these considerations are addressed with the use of the integrative model.

Application of the Integrative Model

Utilizing the integrative model would result in a more holistic formulation, a "psychospirituomoral" formulation. The model would also provide more specific goals, and a more specific and concrete plan for the course of spiritual direction. It would also provide "markers" for informally assessing and monitoring changes over the course of the sessions between Jane and the spiritual director.

Spiritual directors who utilize the integrative model and have internalized the spirituality that it embodies are not likely to sit back and wait for directees like Jane to initiate discussion of difficult and troubling job concerns. By engaging directees in a mutual assessment of the dimensions of transformation, such concerns will invariably surface again or these spiritual directors would find ways of appropriately re-introducing such critical matters. If they were asked: "Is the goal of increased transformation possible if Jane silently avoids dealing with difficult situations, like the pastor's style of relating and his firing of Jane's personnel without due process?" their answer would likely be "No."

The Course and Outcome of Spiritual Direction

Chapter 6 described guidelines for utilizing the integrative model. These included seven strategies for structuring and optimizing the process of spiritual direction and its outcome. This section discusses how the process of spiritual direction would be envisioned for this case in terms of the seven strategies.

Establish a Relationship of Mutuality

The spiritual director would endeavor to create a safe, loving, and prayerful space for Jane to encounter God in their sessions. The director's use of active listening and empathy would foster an atmosphere in which Jane could share prayer with the director and discuss her relationship to God, including her doubts and fears, her spiritual practices, and her life concerns. In the initial session Jane's expectations for spiritual direction would be discussed as well as the structure of the direction, including confidentiality, duration, and frequency of sessions, fee, etc.

Begin an Assessment of the Dimensions of Transformation

Since the overall goal of spiritual direction is to foster transformation, it is useful for the director to orient the directee to the six dimensions of transformation. This sets the stage for mutually assessing the directee's level of functioning in each dimension.

In the course of assessing the six dimensions, Jane came to the realization that the sociopolitical dimension is intimately related and inseparable from the religious/spiritual dimension of transformation. Although it was somewhat frightening for her, she admitted that if she was to grow spiritually she would have to begin facing her job situation and relationship with her pastor. She now wanted to bring these issues into spiritual direction. The assessment of the six dimensions indicated that Jane was functioning reasonably well in the somatic, moral, and intellectual dimensions. Nevertheless, developmental delays or deficits are noted in three other dimensions:

> Affective Dimension: There appear to be delays in the self-capacities of self-acknowledgment and autonomy. Jane seems to have difficulty in coping with crises or concerns without the need to be solicitous and pleasing others in order to maintain self-esteem and avoid rejection. She is also fearful of authority figures and has difficulty acting independently. These factors may help explain her hesitancy in dealing with personnel issues affecting her religious education program, particularly dealing with the pastor. It may also explain why she mentions work related issues but is not receptive to processing them in sessions with the spiritual director.
>
> Religious/Spiritual Dimension: Besides the related self-capacity of autonomy, as noted above, there is no obvious deficit or delay in this dimension. Nevertheless, Jane expressed the desire for deepening her prayer life, presumably to include some type of meditation.
>
> Sociopolitical Dimension: Finally, there appears to be underdevelopment of the self-capacity of critical social consciousness in that she either does not comprehend the seriousness and social consequences of the pastor's apparent abusive style or she is in denial. Since the fired and abused volunteers report to her, she has the responsibility to not only support but also to protect them, a responsibility for which she is failing.

Assess the Level of Development of Virtues, Spiritual Practices, and Self-Capacities

Together the director and Jane assessed the presence or absence of virtue and spiritual practices for the dimensions of transformation with low levels of functioning. Although the director was not a trained psychologist, he felt reasonably comfortable assessing Jane with regard to the thirteen self-capacities based on her self-description, her personal, family, and spiritual history, and his observation of her.

Highlight Deficits in Virtue, Spiritual Practices, Self-Capacities

Based on this assessment of the dimensions of transformation, self-capacities, virtues, and spiritual practices, the director and Jane were able to identify deficits in self-capacities, virtues, and self-practices. Table 7.1 illustrates these deficits, which will become the focus of the pastoral counseling.

Table 7.1: Areas of Focus in Jane's Spiritual Direction

Virtues	**Spiritual Practices**	**Self-Capacities**	**Dimensions of Transformation**
			Somatic
self-care	inner healing prayer	self-acknowledgment, autonomy	Affective
	centering prayer or Christian meditation		Religious/Spiritual
			Moral
			Intellectual
justice, courage		critical social consciousness	Sociopolitical

Specify a Plan

Even though spiritual direction tends to be less structured than either pastoral counseling or psychotherapy, spiritual direction takes a focus and moves toward a goal or goals, even if such goals are not formally articulated but rather are implied by the course that direction takes, sessions are structured, etc. The integrative model provides a map for spiritual journey. This map serves as the basis for formulating and articulating a general plan for the course of spiritual direction. However, in specifying such a plan, the directee and director must remain mindful that God/Holy Spirit is the principal spiritual director and may modify such a plan at any time.

A mutually agreed upon plan which specifies the focus and goals for course of spiritual direction was established with Jane. This plan included work on the virtues, spiritual practices, and self-capacity highlighted in Table 7.1. They decided to focus primarily on the affective, religious/spiritual, and sociopolitical dimensions simultaneously.

> Affective Dimension: Since fear seems to be a central dynamic, spiritual practices aimed at healing of the heart may be needed. This might include prayer for inner healing of the early experiences that engendered her lack of assertiveness and fear.[5] It might also include reframing fear as a prompt or call to personal and spiritual growth rather than as a signal to cower and retreat. Cultivation of the virtues of self-care (and fortitude/courage) will be important. These spiritual practices are initiated and then reviewed to determine if they are sufficient or whether referral for psychotherapy may be necessary. Psychotherapy focused on developing these self-capacities can be quite helpful.[6]
>
> Religious/Spiritual Dimension: Even though she reported that a prior attempt to meditate was unsuccessful, it may be that the assistance of a spiritual director and possibly another method may better suit Jane. Current meditation method, such as the Christian Meditation method as taught by John Main[7] or Thomas Keating's[8] centering prayer, may be quite useful in deepening her prayer life.
>
> Sociopolitical Dimension: Cultivating the virtues of justice and courage are reasonable goals to be incorporated in the plan. As noted above in the Affective Dimension section, efforts to

[5] Francis MacNutt, *Healing,* anniversary ed. (Notre Dame, Ind.: Ave Maria Press, 1999).

[6] James Masterson, *The Real Self: A Developmental Self and Object Relations Approach* (New York: Brunner/Mazel, 1985).

[7] John Main, *Christian Meditation: The Gethsemani Talks* (New York: MedioMedia, 1999).

[8] Thomas Keating, *Intimacy with God* (New York: Continuum, 1995).

> practice fortitude and courage can facilitate the development of the self-capacities of autonomy and self-acknowledgment. Jane might be encouraged to read about and imitate saints and others who overcame their fears and insecurities and were able to manifest justice, fortitude, or courage in difficult situations. Inner healing prayer directed at the source of these fears and insecurities might also be considered.

While some directees may respond to such spiritual intervention, others may require psychotherapeutic intervention. As with the earlier stated plan, which was based on a psychospiritual formulation, this plan, based on a psychospirituomoral formulation, also indicates the value and utility of deepening the client's prayer life. Unlike the earlier stated plan, this plan identifies delays in three self-capacities which are likely to limit the acquisition of the virtues of self-care and justice. It also suggests specific ways of facilitating the process of transformation in these three dimensions. Presumably, a related outcome of this plan is that Jane's image of God will change or enlarge to reflect her emerging capacity and decision to act more courageously and advocate justice in her job.

Implement the Plan

At their first meeting the director proposed a trial period of four additional sixty-minute sessions scheduled on a monthly basis. It was agreed that by the end of this period they would mutually decide whether to continue. At the fourth session they decided to continue and, as of this writing, have been meeting regularly for over three years and plan to continue meeting. As noted above, their focus for the first year or so was on the affective, religious/spiritual, and sociopolitical dimensions simultaneously. After that the focus shifted primarily to the religious/spiritual dimension.

Assess and Monitor Progress

As a result of the initial assessment in the first two sessions, Jane and the director mutually agreed to focus on job issues, particularly the impact that the pastor's actions had on Jane, her teachers, and the congregation. Jane did admit that she had been so stressed and preoccupied by work matters that she had a difficult time with her daily prayers. She was also so distracted when she tried to read the Bible that she had stopped. She was embarrassed to admit that she naively expected that "all these problems would somehow go away" if spiritual direction focused on her prayer life.

During the second session the director asked if Jane had ever experienced a similar situation in her life. After some hesitation, Jane indicated that her father had "conducted a reign of terror" when her mother had decided to return to college when Jane was fifteen. As soon as Jane's mother acquiesced and changed her mind about schooling, her father "calmed down and things seemed to return to normal." She wondered out loud if her initial denial of the pastor's abusiveness and her acquiescent, pleasing behavior with him was similar to her mother's pattern. Discussion ensued about what God might be teaching her through this experience. During the third session Jane noted that the diocese had begun an investigation of parishioner complaints about the pastor, including a lawsuit by the fired music director. Subsequently, the pastor assumed a very low profile with the staff. Predictably, Jane was relieved that "the system was finally working" and pressure on her to bear responsibility for matters seemed to subside. Nevertheless, she did recognize that she had to learn to balance justice with compassion in her administrative role in the parish. In the next few months, the pastor's annual contract was not renewed and he was subsequently replaced.

At the director's suggestion, over the next two years Jane began to practice daily centering prayer and met with a centering prayer group weekly for instruction and mutual support. Spiritual direction also supports her efforts to develop the virtues of self-care, justice, and courage. Inner healing prayer was initiated in the fifth session and Jane subsequently engaged in this prayer on her own thereafter.

In terms of markers of progress, Jane slowly became an advocate for her teachers on a number of matters with the new pastor and the parish board. She was better able to act with both compassion and firmness. Similarly, her prayer life deepened as she continued with daily centering prayer and the group.

Concluding Note

The case study of Jane raised a number of reservations about the current practice of reductionistic approaches to spiritual direction. The initial psychospiritual formulation and plan for the course of spiritual direction that was reported (on pp. 145–6) reflects such a reductionistic approach. Although the stated goals of enhancing prayer life and "increasing autonomy" seemed reasonable, there was no indication of how these would be implemented nor any indication of their likely outcomes. It was speculated that Jane's previous negative experience with meditation might repeat itself unless a different approach was taken, and that efforts to increase her assertiveness with her pastor might actually lead to her dismissal.

Furthermore, the spiritual director's initial assessment of the adequacy of Jane's image of God as a caring grandmother was also questioned. It was suggested that fostering an image of God that was caring as well as just and courageous was more consistent with the anticipated development of self-capacities and virtues. Perhaps the most important reservation concerned Jane's job situation and the accompanying moral considerations. It was suggested that largely because of their training and supervision, many spiritual directors would not have initiated any inquiry discussion of Jane's job issues after she stated that she wanted to focus on her prayer life and not her work life. Of course, if she were to later initiate discussion of her job dilemma most spiritual directors would have been comfortable—and probably relieved—to discuss the matter and its implications for Jane's spiritual and psychological development. Whether many spiritual directors would feel that discussing its moral implications would be consistent with their training is another matter.

Informed by the integrative model, a mutually agreed upon plan for the course of spiritual direction was established with Jane. It included work on the several dimensions of transformation involving specified virtues, spiritual practices, and self-capacities. Because of the immediacy of Jane's work concerns they decided to focus on the affective, religious/spiritual, and sociopolitical dimensions simultaneously. The extended description of utilizing the integrative model's seven guidelines illustrated the value and usefulness of the integrative model over a more reductionistic approach to spiritual direction.

8

An Integrative Approach to Pastoral Counseling: A Case Study

Case material can reveal the theoretical premises and practice patterns in pastoral counseling. A pastoral counseling case is offered here to illustrate the application of the integrative model to a relatively common case. It also shows the value and clinical utility of this model. To safeguard confidentiality actual case material will not be provided. Instead, the case material presented here represents composites of several cases from my clinical and supervisory experience.

Pastoral Counseling with Maggie S.

Initial Presentation

Maggie S. is a twenty-three-year-old nurse who sought pastoral counseling at the urging of a friend. The friend had recommended the pastoral counselor whom she herself had consulted in the past. The pastoral counselor was licensed as a professional mental health counselor and was willing to accept Maggie's behavioral health plan, which allowed ten outpatient sessions per year.

Maggie presented with a four-week history of insomnia, anxiety, decreased appetite, and an exacerbation of irritable bowel syndrome (IBS). The only precipitant she could identify for these symptoms was her recent engagement to Ralph and an upcoming pre-marital evaluation with the pastor of her parents' parish. She felt some apprehension and guilt about this meeting. She reported no family history of psychiatric or substance abuse treatment and denied any previous psychiatric or substance abuse treatment and any prior pastoral counseling or psychotherapy. Her health had been excellent, with the exception of IBS which began when she was eighteen and preparing to leave for college in another state.

Personality and Systems Dynamics

The social and developmental history indicated that Maggie was the older of two siblings, and that her younger brother had recently graduated from college and was now fulfilling a two-year enrollment in the Air Force reserve. Both her parents were alive and well, and were practicing Catholics actively involved in their church. Her father was an executive in an insurance agency and her mother was a nurse but had stopped working when Maggie was born. She never returned to work, even after both her children had completed school. Maggie's family appeared to be relatively stable albeit enmeshed and controlling. Maggie had been a B-student through high school and college and had been working as an emergency room nurse for about nine months. She liked the work but could not adjust to the schedule of being on duty for twelve hours and off for twelve hours four days a week. Compounding this was the fact that Ralph's job kept him out of town for three or four days a week at least twice a month. The result was that she felt alone and abandoned. While Ralph appears to be quite similar to Maggie's father with regard to achievement and control needs, her father stopped his scheduled business travel after Maggie's mother was involved in a car accident and nearly died when Maggie was six. Ralph, like Maggie's father, showered her with much attention when he was not traveling. Her anxiety symptoms, insomnia, and IBS symptoms reportedly worsen when Ralph is out of town.

There is a pattern of previous exacerbations coinciding with stressful events in her life, particularly involving separation-individuation. Her last episode was about eighteen months ago when she was nearing college graduation.

Spiritual Dynamics

A brief inquiry of her religious beliefs and spiritual life revealed her to be, in her words, a "cradle Catholic." Though she always attended church services when she lived with her parents, since she had begun living on her own the past year she registered at another parish and attended services only occasionally. She had been baptized at birth and confirmed at the age of fifteen. Her image of God was that of an attentive but demanding God who is sometimes close and other times far away. Her prayer style was largely formula prayer, and she continued to say a morning and evening prayer.

The Reductionistic Approach to the Case

All approaches to pastoral counseling involve some kind of case formulation and treatment plan. Reductionistic approaches would specify or imply a case formulation that focused only on spiritual-pastoral dynamics, only on psychological dynamics, or on psychospiritual formulations. In Maggie's case, a psychospiritual formulation was specified along with a treatment focus and target goals.

Psychospiritual Formulation

Maggie's symptoms of anxiety and insomnia and the exacerbation of IBS worsen when her fiancé is out of town. These symptoms reflect her inability to be assertive and the demands of her enmeshed family. There appear to be conflicts with separation and individuation, which she does not tolerate or "stomach" very well and are symptomatically expressed.

There also appear to be some shared common dynamics—involving authority and control—among her fiancé, her father, and her image of God. She is terrified of being alone and possibly harbors the secret wish that Ralph will no longer travel, and God will be more present to her when she feels abandoned and unable to cope. This formulation was developed immediately following the first session.

Initial Focus and Goals of Pastoral Counseling

Near the end of their initial session, the counselor suggested a course of short-term, problem-focused pastoral counseling. It would involve ten weekly individual sessions. Both Maggie and the counselor agreed on the following goals for counseling: (1) to reduce her symptoms and (2) to increase individuation in a limited area of her life, i.e., fostering emancipation from her family of origin in terms of the upcoming marriage. Intervention strategies would include active listening, reframing, interpretation, and assertiveness training.

It was further agreed that the number of sessions could be extended if indicated and mutually agreeable to both. The pastoral counselor thought, but did not disclose to Maggie, that the focus of longer-term treatment would be to continue to address the basic dynamics of separation-individuation and those involving authority and control.

In the course of the second and third sessions other aspects of the case emerged. It became clearer that not only was Maggie somewhat ambivalent about the prospects of marriage, particularly if Ralph would continue his job-related travel, but she also manifested considerable fear about the pre-marital sessions since she had heard that "the pastor was from the old school and made it tough for couples who were living together before the ceremony." Apparently, Maggie and her twenty-four-year-old fiancé had been engaged for two months with a wedding ceremony tentatively planned in approximately six to eight months. They had been sexually involved for approximately one year, and five weeks ago she had moved into Ralph's apartment. Because of her family's prohibition about pre-marital sex and cohabitation, Maggie continued to maintain her own apartment with a roommate while living with Ralph.

Presumably, her family was so far unaware that Maggie was leading a "double life." Even though her roommate made excuses for her when Maggie's family called, Maggie fearfully anticipated that sooner or later her parents would learn the truth. She also felt trapped with the way her mother had taken control of the wedding plans. So as not to disappoint her family, Maggie had reluctantly agreed to have the wedding ceremony at her parent's parish church. What she feared most was that the pastor might learn she was living with Ralph and refuse to marry them, and then report the cohabitation to her family.

When asked what she thought the cause of her symptoms to be, she thought a moment and said that she believed it was basically a conflict between values held by her and Ralph, and the values of her parents and the pastor about marriage and cohabitation. When asked what she expected of pastoral counseling, Maggie indicated that she wanted to be relieved of her symptoms and resolve the impending conflict regarding cohabitation that she anticipated with both the pastor and her parents. She believes she has three options, none of which are without consequences. She hoped that the pastoral counselor would help her decide whether to arrange the wedding ceremony in another church with a more "understanding" priest, or to move out of Ralph's apartment and remain celibate until the ceremony, or to tell her parents and the pastor everything about her relationship with Ralph.

Addenda

While many pastoral counselors would not likely assess a client in terms of various developmental stages, i.e., faith, self, and spiritual development, the following developmental stage profile of Maggie is provided for didactic purposes. In terms of

James Fowler's stages of faith development, Maggie would be assessed at the stage of synthetic-conventional faith. At this stage authority is important and the individual's religious beliefs and values could be expected to be largely unexamined. With regard to Robert Kegan's stages of self-development, she would be assessed as moving toward the institutional stage of self. She also appears to be functioning at Daniel Helminiak's conformist stage of spiritual development, in which external authority is important and where beliefs and values are supported by the approval of her significant others. In terms of psychological types, Maggie resembled a Six on the Enneagram. Finally, it appears that Maggie has a relatively low level of self-transcendence as described by Walter Conn.

Reservations About the Reductionistic Approach

In many respects this is a typical pastoral counseling case. Two sets of treatment goals were described. First, two short-term goals were specified: symptom reduction and increasing separation/individuation in regard to the upcoming marriage. Second, two longer-term goals were specified: interpreting and working through basic separation/individuation dynamics, and working through authority and control dynamics, which would be pursued if the client continued in counseling after achieving the first set of goals.

Still, there are some troubling considerations that are raised by the psychosocial formulation and plan. First, the value conflict about cohabitation between Maggie, her parents, and the pastor was not a part of the formulation. It clearly is a concern for this family and would be expected to influence family as well as personal dynamics. It is also a moral concern that is not included in the formulation or plan for the course of counseling.

Second, there appears to be a disparity between the pastoral counselor's formulation and Maggie's formulation, as well as a disparity between her expectations for treatment and the counselor's goals and treatment plan. Furthermore, a possible value conflict about cohabitation and failure to incorporate Maggie's spiritual dynamics into the treatment plan suggest that her experience of pastoral counseling will be only partially responsive to her needs and expectations. Many spiritual direction supervisors advocate the position that matters are not to be addressed unless the client initiates them. Exceptions to this position might be professional ethical guidelines or state laws involving the threat to seriously harm another, e.g. child endangerment, spousal abuse, etc. But what about this situation? The counselor frames it in psychological terms, separation/individuation, authority and control, dependency, lack of assertiveness skills, and enmeshed family dynamics. Maggie's formulation is a moral conflict which is expressed with psychological and somatic symptoms.

Third, Maggie's expectation that the counselor will help her resolve this moral dilemma is even more problematic, since current pastoral counseling theory and practice favors psychological formations and interventions and eschews or downplays moral formulations and interventions. How will the counselor deal with her expressed expectation for treatment?

Fourth, although the pastoral counselor has gathered information on spiritual dynamics, these are not apparently being incorporated into the treatment plan. Why is this?

Finally, the stated goals of counseling and intervention methods seem vague. For example, what exactly is "limited" individuation and what is the target goal of assertiveness training? Would it include telling off the pastor? Furthermore, what "markers" or outcome indicators will the pastoral counselor utilize in monitoring and assessing change? Will there be any "spiritual markers"? Traditional markers such as stages of development—i.e., moral, faith, self, or spiritual development, image of God, spiritual practices, etc.—do not easily translate into targeted treatment goals or a plan of intervention. Similarly, neither these markers nor current theoretical models address what to do about the rather different formations: Maggie's morally-oriented formulation and the pastoral counselor's psychospiritually-oriented formulation. Doubtless, some pastoral counselors would opt for a broader formulation that encompassed elements of both the moral and psychospiritual formulations. But the question still remains: What would they specify as target goals and interventions for the pastoral counseling process?

Application of the Integrative Approach

This case can be formulated in terms of the integrative model. The first step is to make an assessment of the dimensions of transformation. Making this assessment a mutual activity between client and counselor will increase client trust and confidence in the counselor and the counseling process, can facilitate a commonly shared case formulation, and may increase client commitment to achieving treatment goals. It also addresses the first three considerations noted above. The moral conflict in this case is apparent and discussing it in the course of pastoral counseling is essential. Suggesting a referral to a priest-confessor to deal with this moral conflict at the outset of counseling might be at the risk of the client prematurely terminating treatment. It is conceivable that Maggie dismissed the prospect of talking to a priest prior to seeking pastoral counseling.

With the integrative model this case can be formulated in a more holistic and clinically useful fashion, i.e., a psychospirituomoral formulation, than in a psychospiritual formulation. Utilizing the integrative model in this case also addresses the five considerations noted above.

The Course and Outcome of Pastoral Counseling

Chapter 6 described guidelines for utilizing the integrative model. These included seven strategies for structuring and optimizing the process and outcomes of counseling. This section discusses the course and outcomes of this case in terms of these seven strategies.

Establish a Relationship of Mutuality

Utilizing active listening, empathy, and unconditional positive regard the counselor endeavored to engage Maggie in the counseling process. He began an empathic enquiry about her presenting concerns and why she had made the decision to seek counseling now. He carefully elicited her explanation, i.e., formulation, of her concerns as well as her specific expectations for counseling. He acknowledged her morally-based formulation and indicated his willingness to consider all the dimensions of her presenting concern. Then he described the ground rules of the counseling process, the role expectations of both client and counselor, and the importance of mutuality and collaboration between both. Near the end of the first session it was mutually agreed to meet on a weekly basis for ten sessions. The sessions were to be for individual counseling and only include others, such as Ralph or Maggie's parents, if indicated.

Begin an Assessment of the Dimensions of Transformation

Like most individuals on the spiritual journey, Maggie's personal development and spiritual growth was fuller or more mature in some areas than in others. The counselor briefly described each dimension of transformation and involved Maggie in the assessment process. Together they estimated her level of functioning for each dimension. They concluded that she had achieved a reasonable level of development in the religious/spiritual dimension. However, the somatic, affective, moral, sociopolitical, and intellectual dimensions were noted to be less developed.

Assess the Level of Development of Virtues, Spiritual Practices, and Self-Capacities

Together the counselor and Maggie assessed the presence or absence of virtue and spiritual practices for the dimensions of transformation with low levels of functioning. Throughout the initial sessions the counselor observed Maggie with regard to the thirteen self-capacities. Prior to their discussion of treatment focus and goals for counseling, the counselor described his assessment of her self-capacities, emphasizing both strengths and deficits.

Highlight Deficits in Virtue, Spiritual Practices, Self-Capacities

Based on this assessment of the dimensions of transformation, self-capacities, virtues, and spiritual practices, the counselor and Maggie were able to identify deficits in self-capacities, virtues, and self-practices. Table 8.1 illustrates these deficits, which will become the focus of the pastoral counseling.

Table 8.1: Deficits and Areas of Focus for Counseling Maggie

(Other)	**Virtues**	**Spiritual Practices**	**Self-Capacities**	**Dimensions of Trans-formaxtion**
	practice temperance and physical fitness	practice mindfulness in eating	increase self-mastery	Somatic
process psycholo-gical component of guilt	practice self-care	practice reframing fear, consider inner healing work	increase self-acknowledg-ment, self-soothing, and autonomy	Affective
				Religious/ Spiritual
process moral conflict		daily practice of truthfulness	increase capacity for commitment	Moral
	practice prudence and discern-ment		develop greater critical reflection	Intellectual
	practice courage		develop greater critical social consciousness	Sociopolitical

Specify a Plan

Maggie and the counselor mutually agreed on the focus and goals for the initial course of counseling. This plan included working on the virtues, spiritual practices, and self-capacity highlighted in Table 8.1. It also emphasized two other aspects noted in that table: processing the moral conflict about cohabitation and processing the psychological guilt Maggie was experiencing.

By utilizing the integrative model it is possible to establish an initial focus for pastoral counseling and targeted goals. For Maggie, this meant focusing primarily on the moral and somatic dimensions, and following some resolution of the moral conflicts and IBS, anxiety, and insomnia symptoms to shift the focus to the affective and intellectual dimensions.

> Affective Dimension: Beginning with the self-capacities, it would be necessary and useful to focus on three: *autonomy,* since Maggie fears being alone and abandoned, which is suggested by increased symptomatology when Ralph is out of town and she is left alone in their apartment; *self-soothing,* since she appears incapable of soothing painful affects without somatic symptoms; and *self-acknowledgment,* since she is overly dependent on others to modulate her self-esteem. It would be helpful for her to cultivate and practice the virtue of self-care. There are various spiritual techniques that could be considered for developing the spiritual practices of healing the heart and learning to love, but two might be particularly useful. The first is teaching Maggie to reframe fear as an annoying but tolerable inner sensation. The second is inner healing work via daily journaling. The counselor might suggest a format for journaling following a cognitive therapy mode or some other mode. For example, she might first describe strong feelings experienced, followed by the non-adaptive self-talk associated with that feeling, which is then followed by a disputation of that with more adaptive self-talk.
>
> Moral Dimension: The self-capacity of commitment and intimacy seem to be reasonably developed, as do the virtues of trustworthiness and fidelity. However, she is likely experiencing

guilty feelings for violating the norm of her family—and Catholic Church—about the sanctity of marriage. Processing her moral conflict seems to be a key factor here. Perhaps it will lead her to some change in her living arrangement, conversing with her parents, seeking the sacrament of reconciliation, etc. Whatever it be, it is essential that this matter be processed with the pastoral counselor as a moral conflict first, and then, if indicated, as a psychological matter, i.e., psychological component of guilt. As this work on the moral dimension is progressing, the focus can begin to shift to the somatic and intellectual dimensions.

Somatic Dimension: With regard to the self-capacities, it may be useful to focus on self-mastery as she has considerable difficulty controlling her thoughts and affects which become channeled into somatic symptoms, at least in specific circumstances. This suggests that this self-capacity is developed to a certain extent, but is not operative in situation-specific circumstances, as when she feels overwhelmed, abandoned, or not in control. Practicing the virtue of self-care and the daily practice of mindfulness while eating should increase the capacity for self-mastery.

Intellectual Dimension: The self-capacity for critical reflection appears to be underdeveloped. This is not uncommon in families that are enmeshed, hold conservative beliefs, or both. The virtue of prudence is likely to be undeveloped, and thus she can be helped and encouraged to learn a process of discernment for making judgments and decisions. Frequently, providing a client with such a process and encouraging her to use it increases the client's capacity for critical reflection.

Sociopolitical Dimension: It may seem that the moral conflict over cohabitation reflects only the moral dimension. However, this matter extends beyond Maggie's parents and Ralph to the parish, the pastor, and the wider community as well. As such it impacts the sociopolitical dimension to some degree. That many do not recognize this fact is one reflection of an underdeveloped self-capacity for critical social consciousness. Because cohabitation is so widespread today it appears to be normative behavior for couples, who give little short-term and long-term social consequences. In some communities, the decision not to cohabitate may require considerable courage among the couple's subcultures. As such advising the practice of the virtue of courage might be discussed with Maggie.

Implement the Plan

This plan was agreed upon and implemented. In the first four sessions efforts were focused on the affective and moral dimensions focusing on the short-term goal of symptom relief. Her anxiety and insomnia were notably decreased. She had only one flare-up of IBS, which occurred between the second and third sessions. She was able to accept and begin to process the counselor's observation that there was a connection between her insomnia, anxiety, and IBS flare-ups and being alone at night. After the third session Maggie decided to move back into her own apartment. Unlike the situation with Ralph's out-of-town travel, her roommate was in the apartment every night. Furthermore, Maggie's guilt feelings were lessened considerably, particularly after the first meeting she and Ralph had with the pastor to plan the wedding. Sessions five through nine focused on her relationship with her parents. During this time she worked on practices associated with the somatic and intellectual dimensions. During the tenth session, she indicated her desire to continue with longer-term counseling to work more on individuation and authority issues.

Assess and Monitor Progress

Targeted "markers" of progress can be quite helpful in determining growth or change. Here are a number of markers specified by dimensions that were utilized to assess and monitor Maggie's progress in counseling. A useful marker for assessing and monitoring growth in the affective dimension would be the reduction or absence of insomnia and anxiety symptoms when she is alone or feeling conflicted. A useful marker for assessing and monitoring the moral dimension might be the reduction or absence of guilt feelings. Assuming that the focus on the affective and moral dimensions is simultaneously addressed, it is possible that the client will experience a decreased level of conflict and thus reduced symptoms. A useful marker for assessing and monitoring growth in the somatic dimension could be the reduction or absence of somatic symptoms, particularly irritable bowel symptoms, when she is alone or feeling conflicted. A useful marker for assessing and monitoring the sociopolitical dimension—critical reflection and prudence—would be the adequacy of discernment in her decisions and judgments.

The tenth session focused on evaluating progress made. Maggie was free of anxiety, insomnia, guilt feelings, and IBS symptoms. Furthermore, she felt confident about her decision to live separate from Ralph until their wedding. Ralph was initially surprised at her decision, but later indicated that it probably was a good decision for him also, as he found Maggie's symptomatic condition and subsequent irritability quite distressing. She was surprised when he told her that before she began counseling he was having second thoughts about the marriage, wondering if he could endure her symptomatic condition indefinitely.

During the initial course of treatment she engaged in the suggested spiritual practices and practiced and made some progress on the virtues of self-care, courage, and prudence. Practicing discernment in decision-making was quite new for her, as she realized she had never really made decisions on her own before. Her previous decisions had either been based on pleasing her parents or were counter-reactions to her parents' desires. She realized her decision to live with Ralph was one such counter-reaction. She began to understand the social impact of cohabitation and how much she was influenced by the norms of her peers and friends, many of whom were also cohabitating. Her relationship with her parents had improved somewhat. She was less fearful of displeasing them and relieved that she no longer was leading a double life. Although she and Ralph had completed the marriage preparation sessions with her pastor, she decided to put off their wedding date until she felt better about herself and more certain about her future.

She embarked on longer-term counseling that focused on individuation and authority issues. This counseling continued weekly for approximately one year. During this time she gained considerable insight about her early life experiences, her role in her family, her relationship with her parents, especially her father. She better understood the relational patterns in her life, how her symptoms safeguarded her from intimacy and commitment, and how her image of God reflected her early relationship experiences with her father. In time her image of God shifted to that of a kindly uncle. She continued to engage in the suggested spiritual practices and virtues. In time she developed increased capacities for self-soothing, autonomy, commitment, critical reflection, and critical social consciousness. Near the end of this longer course of counseling she decided to call off her relationship with Ralph. Three years after completing counseling she sent a letter to the counselor stating she was doing quite well, had married a co-worker some years ago, and that they had recently given birth to a son. She continued to be in touch with her parents and had become quite involved in the parish in which she and her husband were married.

Concluding Note

The case study of Maggie raises a number of reservations about the current practice of reductionistic approaches to pastoral counseling. The initial psychospiritual formulation and plan for the course of pastoral counseling that was reported reflects such a reductionistic approach. Although the stated goal and intervention method of "limited" individuation and assertiveness training seem to be reasonable at first glance, they are actually quite vague. What exactly constitutes limited individuation? Is the purpose of the assertiveness training to stand her ground about the cohabitation or to tell off the pastor?

Furthermore, the value conflict about cohabitation between Maggie, her parents, and the pastor was not even a part of this psychosocial formulation or plan for the course of counseling. It is clearly a value conflict as well as a moral conflict for this family, which inevitably influenced both individual and family dynamics. There is also a significant disparity between the pastoral counselor's formulation and Maggie's formulation, as well as between Maggie's expectation for counseling (i.e., resolve the moral dilemma) and the counselor's expectation (i.e., focus on psychosocial dynamics). Finally, it is puzzling why the pastoral counselor elicited spiritual practices and dynamics if they were not, in some way, incorporated into the treatment plan.

The case of Maggie is a reasonably good illustration of how the integrative model can be applied to a not uncommon presentation to pastoral counseling. Informed by the integrative model, a mutually agreed upon plan for the course of pastoral counseling was established with Maggie. It included work on the several dimensions of transformation involving specified virtues, spiritual practices, and self-capacities. Because of the immediacy of Maggie's concerns and symptoms it was decided to focus on the moral and somatic dimensions at first, and to focus on the affective and intellectual dimensions following some resolution of the moral conflicts and IBS, anxiety, and insomnia symptoms. The extended description of utilizing the integrative model's seven guidelines illustrated the clinical value and utility of the integrative model over a more reductionistic approach to pastoral counseling.

9

Spiritual Direction and Pastoral Counseling: Some Future Prospects

This concluding chapter highlights the key points of this book. It also points to some emerging trends and suggests some future prospects for the practice of pastoral counseling and spiritual direction.

Key Points

The basic purpose of this book was twofold: to provide a critical analysis of the current theories and practice of pastoral counseling and spiritual direction, and to propose, describe, and illustrate an integrative model for the practice of these two specialties.

Human experience rather than theory was the starting point of this book; specifically, the domains and dimensions of human experience. It was pointed out that the current practice of pastoral counseling and spiritual direction is problematic in several ways and reflects conceptual and practical shortcomings of current theories underlying pastoral counseling and spiritual direction. These shortcomings include: reductionism, particularly the absence or minimization of the moral domain; over-reliance on psychological constructs; the intentional or unintentional promotion of individualism; and practice limitations, i.e., providing few if any practice guidelines and techniques. A final concern is an ethical matter—access and availability of services to the poor—that has arisen as both pastoral counseling and spiritual direction become increasingly professionalized.

Four prominent theories used by pastoral counselors and spiritual directors were reviewed and evaluated: developmental stage theories, image of God theories, psychological types, and self-transcendence theory. In terms of theoretical and praxis adequacy, none held up well to critical scrutiny. All were judged to be conceptually reductionistic since none addressed more than two life domains and were focused exclusively on self-transformation. Even the best studied theories had only marginal research support. Accordingly, they were evaluated to be inadequate as a foundational basis for the practice of pastoral counseling and spiritual direction.

Of these theories, Walter Conn's self-transcendence theory was described as the most promising of current foundation theories of pastoral counseling and spiritual direction. Nevertheless, it emphasized the psychological and spiritual domains at the expense of the moral domain, and focused on self-transcendence—which is similar to self-transformation—at the expense of social transformation.

It was also noted that the current practice of pastoral counseling and spiritual direction is in tension with a number of counterbalancing trends: the re-bridging of moral theology and spiritual theology; the retrieval of virtue ethics; the retrieval of the roots of moral philosophy in scientific psychology; the emergence of systems theory which provides a social and communal balance to the limiting focus on intrapsychic and interpersonal aspects in pastoral counseling and spiritual direction.

Four promising recent developments were also noted. These involve the recent emergence of "positive psychology" and its research agenda focused on the study of virtue; transpersonal psychotherapy with its emphasis on spiritual practices; self-theory with a focus on self-capacities; and transformation with a focus on facets of conversion. These developments suggest a more heuristic framework for the integrative practice of pastoral counseling and spiritual direction.

A case was made that a new foundational model is needed that is integrative, holistic, and also practice-oriented, i.e., providing practical guidelines. Furthermore, it was argued that a fully articulated theory of pastoral counseling and spiritual direction was not possible, until recently, due to the lack of adequate taxonomies and models—the requisite building blocks for an adequate theory.

The proposed model addresses the conceptual and practical shortcoming, or validity checks. It is holistic because it includes and articulates the three domains: the moral domain with the construct of character and virtue; the psychological domain with the construct of self and self-capacities; and the spiritual domain with the construct of spirituality and spiritual practices. It is integrative in that it relates and articulates self-capacities, virtues, and spiritual practices with the dimensions of transformation. Furthermore, detailed case examples involving both pastoral counseling and spiritual direction illustrated its practical guidelines as well as clinical value and utility.

To recap, the proposed model highlights and describes three "markers"—virtues, spiritual practices, and self-capacities—that articulate the constructs of self, spirituality, and character. Since the proposed model forms a conceptual map of transformation in its various dimensions, it provides a useful perspective for understanding and respecting an individual's unique spiritual journey. The map can greatly aid the process of assessing, selecting goals and a focus, planning interventions, and monitoring progress throughout the course of spiritual direction and pastoral counseling.

Emerging Trends and Prospects for the Future

A convergence of trends suggests that the practice of both spiritual direction and pastoral counseling will become increasingly integrative. At least four trends can be noted.

The first is that the disciplines of social, counseling, and clinical psychology are increasingly receptive to the emerging field of "positive psychology" and its emphasis on the experimental study of virtue. Similarly, psychology is also becoming more receptive to both the moral and spiritual dimensions of human experience. Since pastoral counselors and spiritual directors tend to be influenced by emerging trends in psychology, it is quite likely that they will incorporate these developments resulting in a more integrative practice.

Second, there are an increasing number of prophetic voices within both pastoral counseling and spiritual direction advocating the integration of the moral and spiritual domains with the psychological domain. This trend toward integration is occurring simultaneously with the move toward greater professionalization increases the likelihood that professional and ethical guidelines will reflect this trend.

Third, it is unlikely that prospective and ongoing clients will reduce their expectations that clinicians, including psychotherapists, pastoral counselors, and spiritual directors, should deal with not only psychological but spiritual and moral issues in their practice. In fact, it could well be that such an expectation will actually increase.

Fourth, while most pastoral counseling and spiritual direction typically occurs in one-to-one meetings, it is quite likely that in the near future both pastoral counseling and spiritual direction will be increasingly offered in a group context. Given the current interest for incorporating the spiritual dimension in everyday life, spiritual direction in a group context is likely to become more common than pastoral counseling in group settings, thus, the following remarks are focused primarily on spiritual direction. Even though a focus on the individual characterized pastoral care in the twentieth century, many pastorally-oriented writers have advocated that group spiritual direction should be the norm rather than individual spiritual direction. For instance, over twenty-five years ago Adrian Van Kaam insisted that one-to-one spiritual direction should be reserved primarily for crisis situations.[1] Advantages and disadvantages of both individual and group spiritual direction have been detailed.[2] Perhaps the major advantage of group direction is that more individuals will have access to formal spiritual direction. Generally speaking, group spiritual direction can be particularly useful for individuals who will benefit from being exposed to a wide variety of spiritual practices and who can reflect on their own spiritual journey as well as receive feedback and learn from the experiences of others in the group. On the other hand, one-on-one direction can be particularly valuable for individuals undergoing an unusual or difficult spiritual experience or who need or want assistance in discerning a major life decision.

Fifth, it is quite likely that theory development in pastoral counseling and spiritual direction will not only expand but will flourish in the coming years. Existing methodologies such as quality improvement strategies, clinical practice guidelines, and outcomes measurement and management systems, which are currently being used to evaluate the process and outcomes of psychotherapy, group therapy, and marital and family therapy, have already begun to be applied to pastoral counseling in some settings. Such methodologies have been shown to improve process and outcome. Interestingly, these methodologies are also indirectly impacting theory development. For example, the recently reported multi-site study of combined treatment for chronic depression has already begun to change how many clinicians and researchers think about treatment planning, particularly the need for focused and prescriptive psychotherapy.[3] Presumably, these methods can positively impact process and outcomes in both spiritual direction and pastoral counseling as well as theory development.

[1] Adrian Van Kaam, *The Dynamics of Spiritual Self-Direction* (Denville, N.J.: Dimension Books, 1976) 384.

[2] Shawn McCarty, "On Entering Spiritual Direction," *Review for Religious* 35 (1976) 864–5.

[3] James McCullough and Marvin Goldfried, *Treatment of Chronic Depression* (New York: Guilford Press, 1999).

A sixth trend concerns possible directions for future research that could be reasonably pursued. Studies could be designed that empirically test some of the assumptions of this book. One assumption is that training and supervision that is reductionistic fosters reductionistic practice. For example, a study could evaluate the impact of type of training on the ideological orientation and practice patterns of spiritual directors and pastoral counselors. Specifically, it could assess the extent to which training and supervision that focus on individual dynamics in the spiritual journey, i.e., self-transformation, limit or discourage a focus on social and moral concerns and social transformation as compared to training that is more holistic and integrative. A recently published empirical study by John Wall, Thomas Needham, Don Browning, and Susan James provides some indirect support for this assumption.[4] It is interesting to note that Don Browning, the well-regarded author and professor of pastoral counseling, was involved with this research project. The Wall et al. study suggests that counselors and therapists whose training emphasized family systems dynamics were more likely to be sensitive to social and relational ethical or moral concerns than were counselors and therapists whose training emphasized individual dynamics. This study could conceivably be replicated with a sample of pastoral counselors and spiritual directors. Or, a study that more directly tests the assumption of reductionistic theory and training could be done.

[4] John Wall, Thomas Needham, Don Browning, and Susan James, "The Ethics of Relationality: The Moral Views of Therapists Engaged in Marital and Family Therapy," *Family Relations* 48 (1999).

References

Allers, Rudolf. *The Psychology of Character.* Trans. E. B. Strauss. New York: Sheed & Ward, 1931.

Allport, Gordon W. *Personality: A Psychological Interpretation.* New York: Holt, 1937.

Aristotle. *The Nicomachean Ethics.* Trans. with an intro. by D. Ross. Oxford: Oxford University Press, 1951.

Baumeister, R., and J. Exline. "Virtue, Personality and Social Relations: Self-Control the Moral Muscle." *Journal of Personality* 67:6 (1999) 1165–94.

Beauchamp, Tom L., and James F. Childress. *Principles of Biomedical Ethics.* 4th ed. New York: Oxford University Press, 1994.

Billy, Dennis J. "The Unfolding of a Tradition." *Spirituality and Morality: Integrating Prayer and Action.* Ed. Dennis J. Billy and Donna L. Orsuto, 9–31. New York: Paulist Press, 1996.

______, and Donna L. Orsuto, eds. *Spirituality and Morality: Integrating Prayer and Action.* New York: Paulist Press, 1996.

Brown, William P. *Character in Crisis: A Fresh Approach to the Wisdom Literature of the Old Testament.* Grand Rapids, Mich.: Eerdmans, 1996.

Browning, Don S. *A Fundamental Practical Theology: Descriptions and Strategic Proposals.* Minneapolis: Fortress Press, 1991.

______. *The Moral Context of Pastoral Care.* Philadelphia: Westminster Press, 1976.

Bullis, Ronald K. *Spirituality in Social Work Practice.* Washington, D.C.: Taylor & Francis, 1996.

Childs, Brian. "Pastoral Care and the Market Economy: Time-Limited Psychotherapy, Managed Care and the Pastoral Counselor." *Journal of Pastoral Care* 62 (1999) 53, 57–76.

Clinebell, Howard J. *Basic Types of Pastoral Care and Counseling: Resources for the Ministry of Healing and Growth.* Rev. ed. Nashville: Abingdon Press, 1984.

Cloninger, R., D. Svrakic, and T. Pryzbeck. "A Psychobiological Model of Temperament and Character." *Archives of General Psychiatry* 50 (1993) 975–90.

Cohen, Elliot D., and Gale Spieler Cohen. *The Virtuous Therapist: Ethical Practice of Counseling and Psychotherapy.* Belmont, Calif.: Brooks/Cole, 1999.

Conn, Joann Wolski. *Spirituality and Personal Maturity.* New York: Paulist Press, 1989.

Conn, Walter. "Self-Transcendence, the True Self, and Self-Love." *Pastoral Psychology* 46 (1998) 323–32.

Cortright, Brant. *Psychotherapy and Spirit: Theory and Practice in Transpersonal Psychotherapy.* Albany: State University of New York Press, 1997.

Cushman, Philip. *Constructing the Self, Constructing America: A Cultural History of Psychotherapy*. Boston: Addison-Wesley, 1995.

______. "Why the Self Is Empty." *American Psychologist* 45 (1990) 599–611.

Downey, Michael. "Christian Spirituality: Changing Currents, Perspective, Challenges." *America* 170 (1994) 8–12.

______. *Understanding Christian Spirituality.* New York: Paulist Press, 1997.

Drane, James F. *Becoming a Good Doctor: The Place of Virtue and Character in Medical Ethics.* Kansas City, Mo.: Sheed & Ward, 1988.

Dunne, T. "The Future of Spiritual Direction." *Review for Religious* 53 (1994) 584–90.

Edwards, Tilden. *Spiritual Friend: Reclaiming the Gift of Spiritual Direction.* New York: Paulist Press, 1980.

Erikson, Erik. *Identity and the Life Cycle.* New York: International Universities Press, 1959.

Evans, Abigail. *The Healing Church: Practical Programs for Health Ministries.* Cleveland: United Church Press, 1999.

Farley, Benjamin. *In Praise of Virtue: An Exploration of the Biblical Virtues in a Christian Context.* Grand Rapids, Mich.: Eerdmans, 1995.

Flanagan, Owen. *Self-Expressions: Mind, Morals and the Meaning of Life.* New York: Oxford University Press, 1996.

______. *Varieties of Moral Personality: Ethics and Psychological Realism.* Cambridge, Mass.: Harvard University Press, 1991.

Frankfort-Nachmias, Chava, and David Nachmias. *Research Methods in the Social Sciences.* 4th ed. New York: St. Martin's Press, 1992.

Ford-Grabowsky, M. "Flaws in Faith-Development Theory." *Religious Education* 82 (1987) 81–3.

Fowler, James W. *Stages of Faith: The Psychology of Human Development and the Quest for Meaning.* San Francisco: HarperSanFrancisco, 1995.

Frank, Jerome. *Psychotherapy and the Human Predicament: A Psychological Approach.* New York: Schocken Books, 1978.

Frankl, Viktor. *The Doctor and the Soul: An Introduction to Logotherapy.* Trans. Richard and Clara Winston. New York: Knopf, 1955.

Freke, Timothy. *Encyclopedia of Spirituality: Information and Inspiration to Transform Your Life.* New York: Sterling Publishing, 2000.

Galindo, I. "Spiritual Direction and Pastoral Counseling." *Journal of Pastoral Care* 51 (1997) 395–402.

Gelpi, Donald. *Committed Worship: A Sacramental Theology for Converting Christians.* Vol. 1. Collegeville: The Liturgical Press, 1993.

______. *The Conversion Experience: A Reflective Guide for RCIA Participants and Others.* New York: Paulist Press, 1998.

Graham, Larry. *Care of Persons, Care of Worlds: A Psychosystems Approach to Pastoral Care and Counseling.* Nashville: Abingdon Press, 1992.

Gratton, Carolyn. *The Art of Spiritual Guidance: A Contemporary Approach to Growing in the Spirit.* New York: Crossroad, 1992.

______. "The Ministry of Spiritual Guidance." *The Way Supplement* 91 (1998) 17–27.

Gula, Richard. *Ethics in Pastoral Ministry.* New York: Paulist Press, 1996.

Haring, Bernard. *The Virtues of an Authentic Life: A Celebration of Christian Maturity.* Liguori, Mo.: Liguori, 1997.

Hauerwas, Stanley. *Character and the Christian Life: A Study in Theological Ethics.* Notre Dame, Ind.: University of Notre Dame Press, 1975.

Heinrichs, D. "Our Father Which Art in Heaven: Parataxic Distortions in the Image of God." *Journal of Psychology and Theology* 10 (1982) 120–9.

Heller, David. *The Children's God.* Chicago: University of Chicago Press, 1986.

Helminiak, Daniel. *Spiritual Development: An Interdisciplinary Study.* Chicago: Loyola University Press, 1987.

Hillman, James, and Michael Ventura. *We've Had a Hundred Years of Psychotherapy—and the World's Getting Worse.* San Francisco: HarperSanFrancisco, 1992.

Holifield, E. Brooks. *A History of Pastoral Care in America: From Salvation to Self-Realization.* Nashville: Abingdon Press, 1983.

Howe, Leroy. *The Image of God: A Theology for Pastoral Care and Counseling.* Nashville: Abingdon Press, 1995.

Hunsinger, Deborah van Deusen. *Theology and Pastoral Counseling: A New Interdisciplinary Approach.* Grand Rapids, Mich.: Eerdmans, 1995.

Johnson, Susanne. *Christian Spiritual Formation in the Church and Classroom.* Nashville: Abingdon Press, 1989.

Johnstone, Brian. "The Dynamics of Conversion." *Spirituality and Morality: Integrating Prayer and Action.* Ed. Dennis J. Billy and Donna L. Orsuto, 32–48. New York: Paulist Press, 1996.

Jung, Carl. *Psychology and Religion: East and West.* London: Routelage & Kegan Paul, 1958.

Karasu, T. "Spiritual Psychotherapy." *American Journal of Psychotherapy* 53 (1999) 143–62.

Keating, Thomas. *Intimacy with God.* New York: Continuum, 1995.

______. *Invitation to Love: The Way of Christian Contemplation.* New York: Continuum, 1998.

Keenan, James F. *Goodness and Rightness in Thomas Aquinas's* Summa Theologiae. Washington, D.C.: Georgetown University Press, 1992.

______. "How Catholic Are the Virtues?" *America* 176:20 (1997) 16–22.

______. "Proposing Cardinal Virtues." *Theological Studies* 56:4 (1995) 709–29.

______. *Virtues for Ordinary Christians.* Kansas City, Mo.: Sheed & Ward, 1996.

Kegan, Robert. *The Evolving Self: Problem and Process in Human Development.* Cambridge, Mass.: Harvard University Press, 1983.

Kohlberg, Lawrence. *Essays on Moral Development.* New York: HarperCollins, 1984.

Lescher, B. "The Professionalization of Spiritual Direction: Promise and Peril." *Listening* 32 (1997) 81–90.

Lesser, Elizabeth. "Insider's Guide to Twenty-first–Century Spirituality." *Spirituality and Health: The Soul/Body Connection* (Spring 2000) 46–51.

______. *The New American Spirituality: A Seeker's Guide.* New York: Random House, 1999.

Liebert, Elizabeth. *Changing Life Patterns: Adult Development in Spiritual Direction.* Rev. ed. New York: Paulist Press, 2000.

Lomas, Peter. *Doing Good? Psychotherapy Out of Its Depth.* Oxford: Oxford University Press, 1999.

Lonergan, Bernard. *Method in Theology.* New York: Herder & Herder, 1972.

Loewenthal, K. *The Psychology of Religion: A Short Introduction.* Oxford: One World Publications, 2000.

MacIntyre, Alasdair. *After Virtue: A Study in Moral Theory.* 2d ed. Notre Dame, Ind.: University of Notre Dame Press, 1984.

Marinoff, Lou. *Plato Not Prozac: Applying Philosophy to Everyday Problems.* New York: HarperCollins, 1999.

Masterson, James F. *The Personality Disorders.* Phoenix: Zieg/Tucker, 2000.

______. *The Real Self: A Developmental, Self, and Object Relations Approach.* New York: Brunner/Mazel, 1985.

May, Gerald. *Care of Mind, Care of Soul: A Psychiatrist Explores Spiritual Direction.* San Francisco: HarperSanFrancisco, 1992.

McBrien, Richard P. *Catholicism.* New ed. San Francisco: HarperSanFrancisco, 1994.

McCarty, S. "On Entering Spiritual Direction." *Review for Religious* 35 (1976) 854–67.

McCullough, James, with a foreword by Marvin Goldfried. *Treatment for Chronic Depression: Cognitive Behavioral Analysis System of Psychotherapy (CBASP).* New York: Guilford Press, 2000.

McCullough, M., and C. Snyder. "Classical Sources of Human Strength: Revisiting an Old House and Building a New One." *Journal of Social and Clinical Psychology* 19:1 (2000) 1–10.

McCullough, M., and C. Snyder, eds. Special issue on virtues. *Journal of Social and Clinical Psychology* 19 (2000).

Meara, N., L. Schmidt, and J. Day. "Principles and Virtues: A Foundation for Ethical Decisions, Policies, and Character." *The Counseling Psychologist* 24:1 (1996) 4–77.

Merton, Thomas. *New Seeds of Contemplation.* Rev. ed. New York: Norton, 1974.

Millon, Theodore. *Disorders of Personality: DSM-IV and Beyond.* 2d ed. New York: J. Wiley, 1996.

O'Brien, M. "Practical Theology and Postmodern Religious Education." *Religious Education* 94:3 (1999) 313–28.

O'Keefe, Mark. *Becoming Good, Becoming Holy: On the Relationship of Christian Ethics and Spirituality.* New York: Paulist Press, 1995.

______. "Catholic Moral Theology and Christian Spirituality." *New Theology Review* 7:2 (1994) 60–73.

Oliner, Samuel, and Pearl Oliner. *The Altruistic Personality: Rescuers of Jews in Nazi Europe.* New York: Free Press, 1988.

Parsons, Talcott, and Edward Shils, eds. *Toward a General Theory of Action.* New York: Harper & Row, 1962.

Paulsell, S. "Honoring the Body." *Practicing Our Faith: A Way of Life for a Searching People.* Ed. Dorothy Bass, 13–27. San Francisco: Jossey-Bass, 1997.

Pattison, Stephen, and James Woodward. "An Introduction to Evaluation in Pastoral Theology and Pastoral Care." *The Blackwell Reader in Pastoral and Practical Theology.* Ed. James Woodward and Stephen Pattison. Oxford: Blackwell Publishers, 2000.

Poling, J. "Ethical Reflection and Pastoral Care, Part II." *Pastoral Psychology* 32 (1984) 160–70.

Pruyser, Paul. *The Minister as Diagnostician.* Philadelphia: Westminster Press, 1976.

Ranaghan, D. *A Closer Look at the Enneagram.* South Bend, Ind.: Greenlawn Press, 1989.

Reich, Wilhelm. *Character Analysis.* New York: Noonday Press, 1966.

Richardson, Frank, Blaine Fowers, and Charles Guignon. *Re-envisioning Psychology: Moral Dimensions of Theory and Practice.* San Francisco: Jossey-Bass, 1999.

Rieff, Philip. *Freud: The Mind of a Moralist.* Chicago: University of Chicago Press, 1959.

______. *The Triumph of the Therapeutic.* New York: HarperCollins, 1966.

Riso, Don, and R. Hudson. *Understanding the Enneagram: The Practical Guide to Personality Types.* Rev. ed. Boston: Houghton Mifflin, 2000.

Rizzuto, Ana-Maria. *The Birth of the Living God: A Psychoanalytic Study.* Chicago: University of Chicago Press, 1981.

______. "Religious Development: A Psychoanalytic Point of View." Religious Development in Childhood and Adolescence. Special issue, ed. F. Oser and W. Scarlett. *New Directions for Child Development* 52 (1991) 47–60.

Rohr, Richard. *Discovering the Enneagram: An Ancient Tool for a New Spiritual Journey.* New York: Crossroads, 1993.

Rolheiser, Ronald. *The Shattered Lantern: Rediscovering a Felt Presence of God.* New York: Crossroads, 1995.

Seligman, Martin. "Positive Social Science." *Journal of Positive Behavior Interventions* 1:3 (1999) 181–2.

______, and Mihaly Czsikszentmihaly. "Positive Psychology: An Introduction." *American Psychologist* 55:1 (2000) 5–14.

Shelton, Charles. *Morality of the Heart: A Psychology for the Christian Moral Life.* New York: Crossroads, 1990.

Simpkinson, Anne A., and Charles Simpkinson. *Soul Work: A Field Guide for Spiritual Seekers.* San Francisco: HarperCollins, 1998.

Snyder, C., and M. McCullough. "A Positive Psychology of Dreams: 'If You Build It, They Will Come . . . .'" *Journal of Social and Clinical Psychology* 19:1 (2000) 151–60.

Sperry, Len. *Cognitive Behavior Therapy of DSM-IV Personality Disorder.* New York: Brunner/Mazel, 1999.

______. "Leadership Dynamics: Character and Character Structure in Executives." *Consulting Psychology Journal* 49:4 (1997) 268–80.

______. "The Somatic Dimension in Healing Prayer and the Conversion Process." *Journal of Christian Healing* 21:3 & 4 (1999) 47–62.

______. "Spiritual Counseling and the Process of Conversion." *Journal of Christian Healing* 20:3 & 4 (1998) 37–54.

Spohn, William. *Go and Do Likewise: Jesus and Ethics.* New York: Continuum, 2000.

______. "Spirituality and Ethics: Exploring the Connections." *Theological Studies* 58 (1997) 109–23.

Stairs, Jean. *Listening for the Soul: Pastoral Care and Spiritual Direction.* Minneapolis: Fortress Press, 2000.

Stone, Howard. "Pastoral Counseling and the Changing Times." *Journal of Pastoral Care* 53 (1999) 47–56.

Steere, David. *Spiritual Presence in Psychotherapy: A Guide for Caregivers.* New York: Brunner/Mazel, 1997.

Taylor, Charles. *Philosophical Arguments.* Cambridge, Mass.: Harvard University Press, 1995.

Taylor, Sharon. Review of *The Image of God* by Leroy Howe. *Presence: The Journal of Spiritual Directors International* 3 (1997) 73–5.

Thornton, Martin. *Spiritual Direction.* New York: Cowley, 1984.

Tyrrell, Bernard. *Christotherapy II: A New Horizon for Counselors, Spiritual Directors and Seekers of Healing in Growth in Christ.* New York: Paulist Press, 1982.

Van Kaam, Adrian. *The Dynamics of Spiritual Self-Direction.* Denville, N.J.: Dimension Books, 1976.

Wall, J., Thomas Needham, Don Browning, and Susan James. "The Ethics of Relationality: The Moral Views of Therapists Engaged in Marital and Family Therapy." *Family Relations* 48 (1999) 139–49.

Walsh, Roger. *Essential Spirituality: The Seven Central Practices to Awaken Heart and Mind.* New York: J. Wiley, 1999.

Wilber, Ken. *Integral Psychology: Consciousness, Spirit, Psychology, Therapy: A Synthesis of Premodern, Modern and Postmodern Approaches.* Boston: Shambala, 1999.

______. *The Spectrum of Consciousness.* Wheaton, Ill.: Quest, 1977.

Woodward, James, and Stephen Pattison. Preface to *The Blackwell Reader in Pastoral and Practical Theology.* Oxford: Blackwell Publishers, 2000.

Index